END

"Calling all men and women — especially those who are preparing for marriage or have been married for many years!! I found a book that must be read together. *"The Diamond in Your Household of Faith"* is a thorough marriage relationship manual. Well researched and well written, Dr. Weeter has produced a book that lifts the women to the place where God wants them to be—and instructs the men how to help the Lord get that done. After being married for over forty years, I was inspired with fresh revelation of how to encourage and be a true support to my wife.

Here is a book that women have been praying for—and men need to read! Guys, some of you have been frustrated in your marriage. You gripe about your wife and don't know what to do about it. Well, here is the answer. Read this book and you will find out the secret to a healthy, amazing marriage!"

PASTOR GEORGE PEARSONS
Eagle Mountain International Church

" David clearly defines how important marriage is in this book, and how as wedded partners, we help raise each other's value and worth. There is a precious jewel we have been given in marriage. This union is God's glory manifested; and we are responsible and empowered to bring it to it's greatest brilliance, displayed for all to see."

BILL KRAUSE

Business Empowerment Coach and Pastor of Family Community Church

" Mylon and I have known David and Lynn Weeter for over 20 years. We have seen first hand how they live their lives with integrity and faithfulness to the Word. You will be blessed by David's timely teaching on the importance of mutual honor and respect in the marriage covenant. When a husband celebrates God's beautiful design for his wife, he will enjoy the reward of her walking in the fullness of her calling, making them a powerful team for Jesus!"

CHRISTI LE FEVRE

Mylon Le Fevre Ministries

❝ I want you to know that after reading *The Diamond in Your Household of Faith,* I was impressed with your research, your insights and revelation from the Holy Spirit. I do hope that it will get into the hands of those in whom you are targeting and will bring them into a greater sense of appreciation for God's divine plan in the Household of Faith."

DR. JERRY SAVELLE

Founder and President Jerry Savelle Ministries

❝ In Dr. David Weeter's new book, *THE DIAMOND IN YOUR HOUSEHOLD OF FAITH,* the last three words he wrote are, "Shine, diamond, shine." To more completely understand those three words and their context within the pages of what he has written, I strongly encourage you to pick up his book, read it, take notes from it, and then, with faith as your tool, apply the revelation David shares in this powerhouse book to your own life and in your marriage.

As I read through this book, I found myself consistently stopping and taking inventory of my own life and marriage; specifically, my actions toward, the words I speak to, my appreciation for, and the manner in which I cherish the DIAMOND the Lord graciously gave me.

What I most appreciate about *THE DIAMOND IN YOUR HOUSEHOLD OF FAITH* is the obvious amount of prayer and study of the Word of God that David invested into the writing of this book. There is a depth of revelation within the covers of this book that, when applied, can be the game-changer that perhaps you have been believing to show up in your life.

DEAN SIKES

Scripture quotations marked *The Amplified Bible, Classic Edition* are from *The Amplified® Bible*, © 1954, 1958, 1962, 1964, 1965, 1987 by The Lockman Foundation.

Scripture quotations marked *New King James Version* are from the *New King James Version* © 1982 by Thomas Nelson Inc.

Scripture quotations marked *Weymouth* are from the *New Testament in Modern Speech* © 1903 by Francis Richard Weymouth

Strong's Exhaustive Concordance: New American Standard Bible, updated ed., © 1995, by The Lockman Foundation

The Woman Question is by Kenneth E. Hagin, © 1983

The Blessing of the Lord: It Maketh Rich and He Adds No Sorrow With It is by Kenneth Copeland, © 2011

The Diamond in Your Household of Faith

ISBN: 978-1-7341832-0-7

Copyright © 2019 David Weeter
P.O. Box 156
Haslet, TX 76052

Printed in the United States of America. All rights reserved under International Copyright Law. No part of this publication may be reproduced, distributed, or transmitted in any form or by any means, including photocopying, recording, or other electronic or mechanical methods, without the prior written permission of the publisher.

Front cover image by Brian Duffield.

First printing, 2020.

Contact@DavidWeeter.org

DEDICATION

I would like to dedicate this book to four people. First of all, to my Lord Jesus, without Whom I would be hopelessly lost and long since divorced and from Whom I was blessed with my own diamond to cherish. Second, to my precious diamond and the love of my life—my virtuous wife, Lynn. Third, to my beautiful and sweet eldest daughter, Tessa, without whom I would not have had the occasion to press into the Lord regarding the specifics of this revelation. Finally, to my "diamond in the rough." My youngest daughter and princess, Niki. You are so amazing! As you continue to listen to Mom and the Lord's teachings, any roughness will be cut and transformed into the multifaceted diamond that will build your own household of faith. I love you, sweetheart.

The *Diamond*

In Your Household of Faith

Dr. David Weeter

ACKNOWLEDGMENTS

With this being my first book and having never been through this process before, the list of people to which I am so very grateful could go on and on! Thank you to my spiritual father, Kenneth Copeland, for hearing from the Lord and pretty much insisting that I write these things down in book form in order to bless people and strengthen marriages. Thank you Pastor Bill Krause for immediately seeing the need and value for this book and being the first to invest financially into its publishing. Thank you Val Pope for your invaluable insight and information to get me started in the right direction and for your friendship for many, many years. A very special thanks to my editor, Jessica Shook, for your diligence, insight, advice, and counsel…not to mention the transcribing, editing, and all the other "hands on" work you have done on this ministry tool! Finally, thank you to my gorgeous wife without whom I would not even be alive much less have written this book. Your patience with me as well as your unconditional love has produced previously unimaginable peace in my life. It does not yet appear what I will be, but I'm so grateful to you that I'm not where I was when you found me! I love you with all of my heart!

AUTHOR'S NOTE

An extremely important piece of information that I learned from Brother Kenneth E. Hagin was actually something he learned early on in ministry from a Bible theologian he heard speak. This theologian made the statement that, in studying Biblical things, it is very similar to climbing a mountain. When you climb one side of the mountain, you have a spectacular view of certain trees, perhaps streams and rock formations, etc. However if you climb that very same mountain from the other side, it looks completely different. You see different trees, different rocks, and the appearance is quite different. Which view is the "right" view? It depends on which side of the mountain you are standing! Both views are correct for their respective sides!

Particularly when it comes to spiritual things contained in the scriptures, to live in the fulness of the principle and reap the maximum benefits of the acquired understanding, you must become a treasure hunter. I mean you have to hunt under every log, turn over every rock, and look under every leaf!

As you progress through this book, you will notice that we look at several scripture references multiple times. This is no accident nor is it merely a way to take up space. Each time we examine a scripture, we are looking at it from a slightly different angle and extracting another nugget we may have overlooked the first time. We may look under the log of a Hebrew definition or see how it's connected with the stream on the other side of the mountain through a different Biblical comparison. In some instances, there are multiple rocks of religious traditions piled on top of the truth that have to be moved out of the way one stone at a time!

I encourage you to take your time as you go through this book and ask the Holy Spirit, your teacher and guide in all things, to reveal to you even more than what is physically contained in these pages. It is, after all, God Who has joined you and your spouse together, and no one desires your success in every area of your marriage more than He does!

TABLE OF CONTENTS

Endorsements i
Dedication vii
Acknowledgments xi
Author's Note xv
Table of Contents xix
Foreword xxi
Introduction xxv
Chapter 1: The Diamond 1
Chapter 2: The Proverbs 31 Woman 9
Chapter 3: The Rest of the Story 17
Chapter 4: One Word from God 33
Chapter 5: Your New Filter 39
Chapter 6: Taking it to the New Testament 47
Chapter 7: Submission 61
Chapter 8: To the Husbands 77
Chapter 9: The Rich Wife 97
Chapter 10: The Wife—The Warrior 105
Chapter 11: The Power of Togetherness 109
Isaiah 54 Weeter Expanded Translation 121
Confessions and Prayers 127

FOREWORD
By Kenneth Copeland

THE DIAMOND IN YOUR HOUSEHOLD OF FAITH

Twenty years ago, David and Lynn Weeter came into my life. Since then, David has become my personal assistant and travels with me at all times in ministry.

I have known and observed David, Lynn and their children up close and very personal, and watched them raise their children. I have been the beneficiary not only of their knowledge and expertise as chiropractors, but also of their powerful prayers of agreement.

Dr. Lynn Weeter is the virtuous woman in Proverbs 31:10-31—a true example of the woman in this book. She is the diamond in David Weeter's household of faith! She is highly trained and instructs in the military self-defense fighting system called *Krav Maga,* developed for the Israel Defense Forces and also used in personal security.

Ryan, the Weeter's oldest child, finished high school when he was only 15 years old and was already doing college credit classes until he was 18 years old, in preparation for Bible college. How was that possible? Because his already very busy mother was his teacher. That's right! Ryan and Niki were homeschooled. In addition, during that time, Lynn battled and won the VICTORY over Lyme disease in record time.

Maybe now you can see and understand why this is a very important book. It should be required reading for every Christian couple just married or planning to be married.

Men, you need to read about *The Diamond in Your Household of Faith,* and step up. Follow what the Holy Spirit has given the Weeter family, and He will turn your family into a place described in Deuteronomy 11:18-21: "Therefore shall ye lay up these my words in your heart and in your soul, and bind them for a sign upon your hand, that they may be as frontlets between your eyes. And ye shall teach them your children, speaking of them when thou sittest in thine house, and when thou walkest by the way, when thou liest down, and when thou risest up. And thou shalt write them upon the door posts of thine house, and upon thy gates: That your days may be multiplied, and the days of your children, in the land which The LORD sware unto your fathers to give them, as the days of heaven upon the earth."

That's God's promise, and with the help and strength of a virtuous woman, it will come to pass. I know. The LORD Jesus gave Gloria to me April 13, 1962.

JESUS IS LORD!

Kenneth Copeland

INTRODUCTION

In 2018, I was honored to be asked to say a few words at the wedding reception of Ryan, my son, and Tessa—whom I now consider my eldest daughter through the covenant blood of Jesus. When I was asked, there was a considerable amount of laughter. I am still uncertain as to whether this laughter was due to the fact that I was asked *if* I wanted to say a few words or possibly because of the phrase "a few words." Apparently I'm not known for being brief. Of course, I immediately agreed to speak and began to seek the Lord as to what to say.

Let me give a bit of background. Due to unexpected and unforeseen circumstances, Tessa came to live with my wife and I for approximately five months before she and my son were married. My son had already moved to another state where he was attending Bible college, and therefore while she lived with us, I was able to observe her very closely for five months. This is an opportunity that most soon-to-be new fathers don't have.

During the time that Tessa lived with us, she experienced a tremendous amount of stress and pressure in multiple areas of her life. She was pressed in just about every area you could think of, from financial to educational, from work to family situations as well as various other things. There seemed to be an inordinate amount of pressure on Tessa during this time. I had the opportunity to not only observe how she responded, reacted, and dealt with these various situations, but I was also able to see and appreciate the character and application of biblical principles in her life.

With that being said, when I sought the Lord as to what He wanted me to say and minister to my son and new daughter at their reception, the message was two-fold: ministry from the Lord to my daughter, while at the same time encouragement and exhortation to my son as to the place and the value with which he was to honor his new wife.

Immediately, I was impressed of the Lord to talk about diamonds. When He said the word "diamond," I almost began questioning the Lord, "Oh, I see...the stress, but it's a little cliché to talk about how stress produces diamonds." We hear the phrase "pressure makes diamonds" so often that we tend to overlook the significance of the principle behind it. Then He brought Proverbs 31 to my mind. Honestly, I was a little disappointed because I was hoping for something more "fresh." How wrong I was! Just as the Lord does, He took me in a completely different direction, connecting Proverbs 31 to Isaiah 54 in a way I had never seen.

After I shared this revelation with my father in the faith, he encouraged me to write this book. Of course, I went back and studied the scriptures in even more detail. My oh my, how rich and how deep it is, what the Lord has said regarding the gem that is the wife!

Just as God took this revelation from the short words and descriptions that I offered at the wedding reception then proceeded to an even more in depth study of the scriptures, this book will do the same. This book is two-fold: for the wife and for the husband. Whether you are engaged, newly married, or have been married for decades, I believe what is shared in these pages will strengthen marriages and your hearts toward each other.

And so we begin our journey.

CHAPTER 1
THE DIAMOND

On a special March evening, I spoke over my son and his bride a short message God had directed me to share. I thought the message the Lord had given me was specifically for the wedding reception, but little did I know how God was going to develop and use it. As I held my wife's hand that evening, feeling the diamond ring on her finger, I knew God had been preparing us through decades of our own marriage to impart something special into our son and his bride, Tessa—his diamond.

Diamonds are beautiful and strong. They are highly sought after and increasingly valuable. To the world, diamonds could almost become cliché when it comes to marriage. But God is never cliché. He created diamonds as marvelous examples of extreme beauty combined with extreme strength.

To this day, diamonds are the most valuable, precious gems of all of the gemstones. And what does the Bible have to say about gems? Proverbs 31:10 says, "Who can find a virtuous woman? For her price is far above rubies." A diamond's value, their preciousness, and their rarity is far above rubies. *Amplified Bible Classic* says it this way, "A capable, intelligent, and virtuous woman—who is he who can find her? She is far more precious than jewels and her value is far above rubies or pearls." This virtuous woman is the diamond in your household of faith.

> *This virtuous woman is the diamond in your household of faith.*

If the value of a diamond is far above the value of all the other gemstones, we can infer the diamond is over all the other gems. Isaiah 54:11 says, "I will set your stones in fair colors [in antimony to enhance their brilliance] and lay your foundations with sapphires. And I will make your windows and pinnacles of [sparkling] agates or rubies, and your gates of [shining] carbuncles, and all your walls [of your enclosures] of precious stones" *(AMPC)*.

When it says foundations, windows, gates, and walls, it is literally talking about your home and your

Chapter One: The Diamond

household! These gems in your household are what the master gem—your diamond—will be over. These are the gems that the Lord furnishes your diamond with to build a household. Your home and your family are designed, built, and equipped with each of these gems, and the diamond is set at the top.

In fact, at the beginning of the verse, the Lord talks about the "setting" of the jewels. The setting has two primary purposes. First, the setting is to enhance the stone's brilliance. A high quality diamond has many facets, therefore the setting is important to the appearance of the diamond. The many facets affect the reflection and refraction of light, therefore the color and purity of the setting affects the color and appearance of the diamond itself.

Verse 11 says to set the stones "in antimony to enhance their brilliance." This refers to how the Egyptian women would use powdered antimony as eye make-up which, when applied around the eyes, made the appearance of their eyes stand out.

The second purpose of a jewel's setting is a functional purpose. Particularly when choosing an appropriate setting for a valuable gem, such as a diamond, it is vital to select a setting which keeps the stone secure in its location. If the setting is damaged or weakened, you run the possibility of losing a highly valuable asset.

Notice what the scripture says will happen when the diamond is in its proper setting:

"And all your children shall be disciples [taught by the Lord and obedient to His will], and great shall be the peace and undisturbed composure of your children. You shall establish yourself in righteousness (rightness, in conformity with God's will and order): you shall be far from even the thought of oppression or destruction, for you shall not fear, and from terror, for it shall not come near you."

Verse 13 begins with the conjunction "and." A conjunction takes what comes before it and connects it with what follows. Therefore, when the stones and gems are in their place, when the diamond is brilliantly and securely set, when the foundations, windows, gates, walls, and borders are laid with their gemstones, *then* all of your children shall be taught of the Lord and be obedient to His will. *Then* great shall be the peace and undisturbed composure of your children. *Because* you establish yourself in righteousness, you will be far

Chapter One: The Diamond

from even the thought of oppression or destruction at that time, for you shall not fear, and terror shall not come near you.

So what setting will enhance the diamond's brilliance and keep it secure? In other words, what is the proper place in the home for the wife? This question has been incorrectly divided from the Word of God for centuries. We are told to rightly divide the Word (see 2 Timothy 2:15), and this particular subject has been so unrighteously divided by religion that it has caused a tremendous weakening of the household, the home, and consequently, of the protection, deliverance, and salvation of the people who make up those homes.

It is true, because of the natural order in the physical realm on this earth, that the husband is placed as the head and covering of his wife—that's what head means, the leader, the covering, the

> *Because you establish yourself in righteousness*
>
> *...*
>
> *you shall not fear, and terror shall not come near you.*

protector. (See Ephesians 1:22, 5:23–29.) However, as we will see, it becomes clear that the wife is at the head of the functioning of the home.

All families have an aspect of business to them. There are certain things that must be handled. Timetables need to be run. The kids need to go to school, practices, and appointments. Groceries have to be bought. Household items need to be secured. There are certain logistical operations of every home. Essentially a family is an institution of humans that has to be organized.

People like to think that a "loving family" only needs it's members to love one another and everything else will fall into place. That may be partially true. Love is the power that makes everything work. But there are a multitude of logistical issues in a family that have to be dealt with. This means a wife must be multifaceted.

Think about the cut of a diamond. The diamond's cut is a style used when shaping a diamond for polishing.[1] An example would be the highly-valued "brilliant cut." The brilliant cut is a diamond cut into a shape with numerous facets to create exceptional brilliance through the gemstone. The multifaceted cut provides maximum light return through the diamond so that it's shine is magnificent.[2] Did you catch the significance of that?

The most desirable and valuable diamonds—including the one in your household—are multifaceted so as to provide maximum *light* return!

As you continue this study, keep this principle of the multifaceted cut in mind.

In the next chapter, we will dig into the Word of God as it shows us exactly how to determine the proper setting and many facets of the God-ordained family.

---

1 https://en.wikipedia.org/wiki/Diamond_cut
2 https://en.wikipedia.org/wiki/Brilliant_(diamond_cut)

CHAPTER 2
THE PROVERBS 31 WOMAN

Unfortunately, the vast majority of the body of Christ has no idea what God's description of a wife really is. They even read Proverbs 31 all the time and still have no clue. There are books and messages galore about the Proverbs 31 woman, but as we dive into the subject of a "virtuous woman," you may be shocked by what it actually means. The majority of these teachings are vastly incomplete at best and blatantly incorrect at worst.

If you ask the average member of any church what the characteristics of a virtuous woman are, most of the time you will hear words such as "chaste, timid, quiet, meek, godly, pious, soft-spoken." But what does *virtuous* really mean? In Hebrew, which is the language used to write the book of Proverbs, virtuous means: "a force, whether of men, means or other resources; an army, wealthy, virtue, valor, strength, able, activity, army, a band of soldiers, or a company; great forces, goods, host, might, power, riches, strength, strong, substance, train as in training of a soldier, valiant, valor, virtuous, war, and worthy."

Did you hear anything indicating soft-spoken, demure, quiet, pious, or chaste? Those words aren't there. As a matter of fact, this very word translated *virtue* is the same word that was used to describe David's mighty men of *valor*. (See 2 Samuel 23.) The words *valor* and *virtuous* used are translations of the exact same Hebrew word. That is how God describes a wife!

No wonder her price is far above rubies. No wonder she's the diamond.

As we go through the rest of Proverbs 31, we'll see God describing the details of what this virtuous woman looks like.

"The heart of her husband doth safely trust in her, so that he shall have no need of spoil. She will do him good and not evil all the days of her life" (vv. 11–12). You can trust someone who is worthy and full of valor and strength. They're powerful. They have great might. They are a force of resources and means. You can trust in someone like that.

"She seeks wool, and flax, and works willingly with her hands. She is like the merchants' ships; she brings her food from afar" (vv. 13–14). If she fits this definition then she is rich. She has the means, resources, and ability to do these things.

"She considers a field, and buys it: with the fruit of her hands she planteth a vineyard" (v. 15). She can do so because she's rich, successful, and hard-working.

We can't skip over verse 17, "She girds herself with strength, and strengtheneth her arms." I like what my spiritual father says, "She ain't no chicken woman." She's strong. She is not scared of anything.

> *...virtuous means: "a force, whether of men, means or other resources...*

Men like to quote Job 38:3, "Gird up now thy loins like a man," and 1 Corinthians 15:13 where it talks about acting like a man. But right here in Proverbs 31:17, the virtuous woman girds *her* loins with strength and strengthens her arms.

"She perceives that her merchandise is good." She makes good choices and does things with excellence.

"She stretches out her hand to the poor" (v. 20). She has plenty of money to give to the poor, and she is generous in doing so.

"All her household are clothed with scarlet. She makes herself coverings of tapestry; her clothing is silk and purple" (v. 21–22). In the context of the day, these were exquisite, fine raiments.

"Her husband is known in the gates, when he sits among the elders of the land" (v. 23). This is the description of the ideal family as God intended. In this age of social media, people often point their finger and say, "Those people just post the good things. You never know what's going on behind the scenes. They make themselves look like the perfect family." Well, such a thing *does* exist and it is described in several places in the Bible. This is our goal! We should always be reaching toward the prize that is set before us in places like Proverbs 31 where it lists what the family is supposed to be like.

"She makes fine linen, and sells it" (v. 24). She knows how to turn a profit.

"She delivers girdles unto the merchant. Strength and honor are her clothing" (vv. 24–25). That strength and honor is inherent to the definition of the word *virtuous*.

"She opens her mouth with wisdom; and in her tongue is the law of kindness" (v. 26). There's a saying that I've heard and spoken often, "One word from God can change your life forever." The virtuous woman can speak a word from God in your life and change things.

"She looks well to the ways of her household, and eats not the bread of idleness. Her children arise up, and call her blessed; her husband also, and he praises her" (v. 28). Men, listen up. Her husband praises her! He doesn't deride her. He doesn't embarrass her. He lifts her up and praises her.

"Many daughters have done virtuously, but thou excellest them all" (v. 29). These are the daughters taught by a virtuous woman. Elder women are supposed to teach the younger according to the book of Titus. (See Titus 2:3–4). "Favor is deceitful, and beauty is vain: but a woman that fears the Lord, she shall be praised. Give her of the fruit of her hands; and let her own works praise her in the gates" (vv. 29–30). Not only will the virtuous woman who fears the Lord have favor and beauty, but she shall also be praised.

Remember in the last chapter, one of the attributes of a diamond that determines it's value is a multifaceted cut. It is no coincidence that Proverbs 31 seems to be describing some sort of Wonder Woman superhero!

She is multifaceted and therefore highly valuable. From manufacturing to real estate, from physical fitness and ferocity to shipping and exports, there seems no end to her God-ordained abilities and anointing!

CHAPTER 3
THE REST OF THE STORY

While Proverbs 31 is well-known for addressing a virtuous woman, until I began deeply studying, I did not realize Isaiah 54 is also addressed to a woman. Verse 1 says, "Sing, O barren, thou that didst not bear; break forth into singing, and cry aloud, thou that didst not travail with child." Then in verse 6, "For the Lord has called thee as a woman forsaken and grieved in spirit, and a wife of youth, when thou wast refused, saith thy God."

Now, I understand God is talking to a people, and He is using the comparison of a woman. But He never uses a comparison that is not valid. That would be ridiculous, and we do not serve a ridiculous God.

The woman described in Isaiah 54 has experienced a great amount of pressure and distress. She has been forsaken and grieved in spirit. Even as a young wife, she was refused (v. 6). But God reassures her, "with everlasting kindness will I have mercy on thee, saith the Lord thy Redeemer" (v. 8). We are the redeemed of the Lord.

She has been "afflicted, tossed with tempest, and not comforted" (v. 11). It sounds like wave after wave has continued to hit her. Have you ever felt like that? You just got up from one wave tossing you around when another hit you from the backside. It makes no difference to God what this woman has been through or even her current situation. The Lord can use her to build something beautiful!

💎 The Stones 💎

Then, as we saw in chapter one, the Lord says, "Behold," (or "Pay attention,") "I will set your stones." This time we're going to pause here. The word *stones* indicates "to build." Notice, "I will set your stones in fair colors [(I will set them) in antimony to enhance their brilliance]." As the diamond in the household of faith, the wife builds with and uses the precious stones at the Lord's instruction, He will take them and offset them in a way that will show the world their brilliance and shine.

◈ The Foundation ◈

Now look at this! One of the definitions of the word *foundations* in verse 11 is "to sit down together." It means "to consult, to establish, to instruct; ordain, to set, and make sure." Listen, you diamonds, *you* are the foundation of your home, your particular household of faith. You are ordained by God to be such, and it is set, made sure, and established by Him.

God is laying the foundations of your family, and He is using these gems under the master stone, the diamond herself. Notice He uses the example of sapphires in verse 11. When you look sapphires up in Strong's Concordance, the Hebrew meaning is "a gem used for scratching other substances." The root word even means "to score or inscribe with a mark as a record." You are to mark your household. It also means "to declare." Wife, you are to inscribe the foundations of your home by declaring the Word of Almighty God over your household, your home, and your family.

When Brother John Osteen was here on earth, he saw a vision where the devil was walking down the streets of a neighborhood followed by his impish demons. As he was walking, the devil pointed to a house, and a couple of the little demons ran off to cause havoc in that house.

That house was marked. It was inscribed in the very foundations of that household by the Word of God.

A few steps later, there was another house, and he sent a couple demons in that house. The rest of the little demons jumped around, excited to get to work on the next house. As they passed this one house, a little demon looked up at the devil and said, "How about that house? Let us go into that house."

They started to head that way, but the devil grabbed them, pulled them back, and said, "No, no, no! Don't ever go into that house. The people in that house are children of the Almighty God and they know who they are. Don't ever go in there. They will beat your brains out."

That house was marked. It was inscribed in the very foundations of that household by the Word of God. The diamond of that household had made certain the house was marked in the spirit, and it was off limits to the devil.

❖ The Windows ❖

It is amazing to me, and it is just like God, that in describing the multifaceted diamond in the household of faith, He uses descriptive words that are also multifaceted.

"I will make your windows of agates, and thy gates of carbuncles" (v. 12). *Windows* has several different meanings. One meaning is "brilliant; a ray" as in a ray of light. But it *also* means "a notched battlement." This word indicates a place in a fortress, notched out to wage battle. The verse says, "windows of agates." *Agate* means "deep." You should have deep, clear vision.

Now pair that together with what we learned about the virtuous woman. Remember, the value of a diamond is determined in part by the clarity of that diamond. The more clear it is, the higher the value. The diamond should have clear vision—brilliant, bright rays of deep vision for her family and the call of God on her family. This clarity of vision is a notched space of battlement through which to overcome all the attacks of the enemy.

💎 The Gates 💎

"And your gates of carbuncles." *Gate* can mean "to act as a gate keeper." My dear diamond of the household, you are to be the gatekeeper of your home. Pray in the spirit. Hear from God and be aware of what is trying to come into your home. You get to decide whether something enters your home or whether it does not. You are the gatekeeper.

The word *gates* is interesting because it also means "to estimate and to think." You should be thinking about your household, the functioning of it as well as the spiritual aspects of it.

These gates are made of carbuncles. *Carbuncle* comes from two root words: *'eqdach* meaning "a fiery gem," and *'eben* meaning "to build." This is fascinating to me for two reasons. First, He is reinforcing the idea of building the home yet again. Second, sometimes when the enemy is trying to gain access to your home, it is necessary to be a firey gatekeeper.

❖ The Borders ❖

"And all your borders of pleasant stones." That word *borders* means "a boundary, a territory enclosed; to bound as with a rope." The root word in the Hebrew means "a twisted rope." And a three-stranded cord is not easily broken. (See Ecc. 4:12.)

If the idea of the foundation means to sit down together, then as you, your spouse, and the Lord grow and work together, that three-stranded cord will *never* be broken. That is your border that will enclose your territory which you have marked by declaring the Word of God over it. It is no wonder the Lord calls the diamond far more precious than rubies or pearls or any other gemstone. "Your borders are of pleasant stones." That word *pleasant* means "valuable, pleasurable, and to be desired."

All of these definitions that we've looked at in Isaiah 54 and Proverbs 31 describe excellence. They speak of wealth, prosperity, value, something to be desired.

Again, the word *stones* in verse 12 means "to build." Notice that it is at the description of the parts of the house, reinforcing the fact that the aforementioned items are to go into building your home. Once these things are in place and your home is built securely, *then* "all your children shall be taught of the Lord; and great shall be the peace of your children" (v. 13). *Because* your home is established in righteousness, "you shall be far from oppression; you shalt not fear: and from terror; for it shall not come near you." Your home is built well. It is secure. The Lord God has laid the gems under your watchful direction. You are a virtuous woman full of power, might, and strength.

Fear and terror may gather together and try to stir stuff up, but they will not come near you. They'll fall for your sake. You've tended to business. You've got all your subordinate stones in place. The devil will roam around as a roaring lion, seeking whom he may devour (1 Peter 5:8), but he cannot devour you because no weapon formed against you shall prosper, and every tongue that shall rise against you in judgment shall be condemned (Isaiah 54:17). This is your heritage. Be the diamond in your household of faith.

Don't get me wrong, you may see the lion roaming and the fear gathering. Remember, Psalm 23 says the enemies are still present and your mind may be screaming that the weapons *are* prevailing against you, but you are a diamond. You are strong by your very nature! Make your declaration and stand (Ephesians 6:13).

❖ WHO IS BUILDING YOUR HOME? ❖

When the Lord first started talking with me about this, I couldn't understand why He was directing me toward the woman being the diamond when it was obvious reading these verses that the Lord was laying the foundation and building all the pieces. He is the One talking in Isaiah 54 when it says, "For the Lord hath called thee," and all the way through to verse 11, "behold, I will lay thy stones with fair colors."

Even in Psalm 127:1, it says, "Except the Lord build the house." So yes, the Lord is building the house here just as we saw in Isaiah. But don't stop reading. The rest of the verse says, "They labor in vain that build it." The cross reference in the *King James* shows the Hebrew translation of the phrase "that build it" meaning "that are builders of it, in it." So here we see the Lord builds the house and if the Lord isn't a part of building it, then those who are attempting to build on their own are doing so in vain.

Think of it as a builder/subcontractor relationship. The Lord is like the builder ordaining and planning everything for the house to be built. Then the subcontractor handles all of the labor. In Proverbs 14:1, God says, "Every wise woman buildeth her house." Women are the subcontractors, laboring to build the home using the blueprints the Master Builder has laid out.

The word *build* in both Psalm 127:1 and Proverbs 14:1 is *banah,* which is the exact same Hebrew word translated *stones* in Isaiah 54:11. "I will lay thy stones with fair colors." The same word is used when God "builds" the house and when a wise woman "builds" her home. It means "to build, to obtain children, to make, to repair, to set up."

> *God gave us His Word as the blueprint to build our household...*
>
> *He knows how to build a household of faith.*

Notice, the meaning "to repair." So even if some things have gone wrong, it's not too late. God can and will repair the household of faith.

Banah also means "surely." It's steadfast, strong, and secure. It creates a sure foundation when the diamond builds her household with the Master Builder.

We see the Lord as the Builder in Isaiah 48:13, "Mine hand also has laid the foundation of the earth, and my right hand has spanned the heavens: when I call unto them, they stand up together." And also in Isaiah 51:13, "And forgettest the Lord thy maker, that has stretched forth the heavens, and laid the foundations of the earth." So where is the diamond's place in the building process? "I have put my words in your mouth, and I have covered thee in the shadow of my hand, that I may plant the heavens, and lay the foundations of the earth" (Isaiah 51:16). God gave us His Word as the blueprint to build our household. We have already seen that He can lay the foundations of the entire earth and span the heavens, so we can rest assured that He knows how to build a household of faith.

Let's step back and look at the whole picture together. "He will lay the foundations with sapphires." Remember, the sapphire is used to scratch other substances and to make a mark for record. In the *Strong's Concordance,* the same Hebrew word *caphar* translated *sapphire* can also mean "talking about, declaring, speaking, and talking." So the wife lays the *foundation* with sapphires marking the substances around the household by declaring, speaking, talking, and writing.

What is she supposed to declare, speak, talk, and write? The whole process is right there in the word foundation: "to sit down together, consult, take counsel, establish, give instructions, ordain, set it and make it sure." The diamond sits down together with the Father, gets His Words, and she declares them, speaks them, talks about them, and marks her household off limits to Satan.

As you put this into action, the foundation of your household of faith will be strong and secure.

💎 Isaiah 54 Expanded 💎

Putting together the definitions that we have read and what we have studied, I have written what we can call the Weeter Expanded Translation of these verses in Isaiah 54. (An expanded version of the entire chapter is written and included in the back of this book.) Based on what we have studied, here is what I believe God is saying to the diamond through these verses in Isaiah 54:

> "You and I are going to sit down together and I am going to personally share My wisdom, insight and understanding with you. I am going to show you how to build the most beautiful and successful life and home that you can imagine. You will have to do the building but don't worry, I have the master plans and blueprints showing you exactly what to do every step of the way.
>
> "I will give you the words that you will use to lay the very foundations of your home, raise up the walls, and install the windows! You will use the power and authority in My words by declaring them to build impregnable gates and borders that no enemy can breach. I'll show you how to mark your territory. You will indelibly engrave your borders and gates

with My mark with your declarations and then defend your territory with whatever firepower necessary to overcome any foe who would dare attempt to enter without your permission. I have equipped you with everything needed to build your home in such a manner to where it is an impenetrable fortress."

CHAPTER 4
ONE WORD FROM GOD

I marvel at how the Word of God weaves pieces together and makes a fabric of truth. In one word the Lord can say a multitude of things. When we are able to take a scripture and dig in further to the original meanings of the words in the text, the scripture become even more rich. That is when we see exactly what the Lord is telling us in His Word.

We have determined what the diamond of your household looks like, but a wife is not automatically this diamond. These scriptures have to be obtained and implemented by faith. For example, "Whoso findeth a wife findeth a good thing, and obtains favor of the Lord" (Proverbs 18:22). Well, only if he finds a good wife. Remember how Proverbs 31 asks, "A virtuous woman, who can find her?" Not every woman is virtuous. Not every wife is a good thing. Proverbs also says, "It is better to dwell in the corner of the housetop than to share a house with a disagreeing, quarrelsome, and scolding woman" (25:24 *AMPC*) or "faultfinding woman" (21:9 *AMPC*).

But for those women who lay hold of these biblical descriptions of what they should be and implement them by faith into their lives and character, they will become diamonds.

Digging in to these scriptures, let's look at Proverbs 18:22, "Whoso findeth a wife findeth a good thing, and obtains favor of the Lord." The Hebrew word used in this verse that translates as *good* is speaking of good in the widest sense of the word. It can be used as a noun, an adjective, or an adverb. It is singular or plural as in, "It is the good, goods, or good things." This word means "beautiful, best, better, bountiful, cheerful, at ease, fair, be in favor, fine." Women, it is good to be fine!

In one word, the Lord shows the most wonderful, glorious description of the facets of a wife. *Good* also means "gracious, joyful, kind; to be liked; to be loving; most pleasant." It means "to be ready." Now I'll just leave that interpretation up to you! Being *good* includes "pleasure, precious, prosperity." Now that is the definition of good, and it's how the Lord describes a wife. Whoever finds a wife, finds a good thing.

Let's read Proverbs 19:14, "House and riches are the inheritance of fathers: and a prudent wife is from the Lord." It doesn't say that an imprudent wife is from the Lord. No, a prudent wife is from the Lord. Again, in one word the Lord reveals to us so much. The root word *sakal* translated as *prudent* means "intelligent, an expert, to instruct, to prosper; to deal prudently, skillful." These meanings sound familiar, don't they? They are almost identical to the meanings of virtuous. A virtuous wife is a prudent wife.

> *But for those women who lay hold of these biblical descriptions of what they should be and implement them by faith into their lives and character, they will become diamonds.*

Reading further into the definition, *sakal* also means "to have good success, to teach, to have understanding and to make to understand." This is where "all of your children shall be taught of the Lord and the elder woman shall teach the younger." Don't you love how the Word weaves together? To have understanding or to make to understand is wisdom. A prudent wife has *wisdom* to teach and to be successful.

Ladies, if you only took those two words *good* and *prudent* as characteristics to grab hold of by faith and make a part of your character, you would become the diamond in your household of faith!

Men, I don't see any possible way that you can read even a single paragraph of this book (with any sense whatsoever of the gift that God has given you) without an overwhelming sense of gratitude, thanksgiving, and value of this precious diamond with which the Lord God Almighty has blessed you.

CHAPTER 5
YOUR NEW FILTER

We have already discovered the true meanings of a virtuous woman, a good wife, and a prudent wife. When you're reading the Bible, keep these words with their full meanings as a filter through which you read scriptures regarding wives. Don't let religious tradition blind you and cause you to slip back into the old traditional way of thinking of meek, mousy, pious, quiet, wimpy women that religious tradition has brainwashed men into thinking. Renew your mind, ladies and men, to the virtuous woman, the good wife, the prudent wife.

◈ Wives of Unbelieving Husbands ◈

Often times the wife is pursuing the Lord before her husband has become a believer. The topic of how she is to win over her husband for the Kingdom of God has also been misconstrued. In 1 Peter 3:1, he is talking to you, virtuous, good, prudent wives when he says, "Likewise, you wives, be in subjection to your own husbands; that, if any obey not the word, they also may without the word be won by the conversation of the wives." The conversation of the wives can not only be how they talk—remember, the household is built by declaring and talking the Word—but also the manner of the wife's life.

For many years, these scriptures have been interpreted that the wife's manner of life and subjection to her husband meant that the wife was to always give in to her husband to the point of being used as a doormat, and that somehow her manner would win over her unbelieving husbands. Not so! If she is a true virtuous, prudent, and good woman, then her success, her strength, her prosperity, her excellence, and ability to run the household well, responsibly, and efficiently is going to win over her unbelieving husband.

❖ Adornment of the Heart ❖

Without the filter of the true meanings of what God calls a good wife, it is common to misunderstand scriptures speaking to women. This is why we must not only read the Word, but study it.

Chapter Five: Your New Filter

Let's look at one of the most misunderstood passages in the entire New Testament, 1 Peter 3:3–5:

> "Whose adorning, let it not be that outward adorning of plaiting the hair, and of wearing of gold, or of putting on of apparel; But let it be the hidden man of the heart, in that which is not corruptible, even the ornament of a meek and quiet spirit, which is in the sight of God of great price. For after this manner in the old time the holy women also, who trusted in God, adorned themselves, being in subjection unto their own husbands."

Even when the scripture points us back to the Old Testament for the example of a wife saying, "in the old time," so many of us still miss it! But throughout this book we have studied and learned what God actually said a wife is to be, so our eyes have been opened and we have a new filter.

Too many people have tried to make doctrine out of scriptures like, "Whose adorning let it not be that outward adorning of plaiting the hair, and of wearing of gold, or of putting on of apparel." But wait a minute.

Religious doctrines haven't known what to do with the last part of that sentence. If you are not going to plait the hair or wear gold as the scripture says, then you must be free to go around naked all the time too. Obviously, we can't do that. That doesn't fit with the rest of the religious stances either. So they ignore that last statement and pretend it's not there. Well, we're not going to do that.

Instead, let's read the *Weymouth Translation* of 1 Peter 3:3, "Your adornment ought not to be a merely outward thing—one of plaiting the hair, putting on jewelry, or wearing beautiful dresses. Instead of that, it should be a new nature within—the imperishable ornament of a gentle and peaceful spirit, which is indeed precious in the sight of God."[3] Now that clarifies it in a new way. Outward adornment is only one part; the renewing of the inward man is also important to God.

But keep reading in this translation. "For in ancient times also this was the way the holy women who set their hopes upon God used to adorn themselves, being submissive to their husbands" (v. 5, *Weymouth*). It is the wife's responsibility to adorn themselves in submission

---

3 Weymouth, Richard Francis. Weymouth New Testament in Modern Speech. Harrison House, 2012.

to their own husband. In other words, how they look and what they wear or don't wear is between the wife and her husband—and nobody else. We have no right to judge or speak against someone else. Keep your mouth shut. Let the woman dress in the manner in which she and her husband thinks she looks pretty.

One other thing I want to point out is in 1 Peter 3:4, "But let it be the hidden man of the heart, in that which is not corruptible, even the ornament of a meek and quiet spirit, which is in the sight of God of great price." Some of those words can be found in the definition of a good wife as we looked at in the last chapter. Again we see that the wife is "of great price," or far more valuable than rubies or other gemstones. She is indeed the diamond in your household of faith.

> *how they look and what they wear or don't wear is between the wife and her husband—and nobody else.*

"Great price" can also mean "extremely expensive." I hear you laughing as you read that! We are not discussing whether or not having a wife is extremely expensive in this particular book, however tempting and humorous the subject could be! The point I am making here is that she is of great value in the sight of God.

Let me put that into perspective for you. We're talking about God, who has gold streets—not gold-plated streets but streets of pure gold. His front gate is not lined with pearls but made of pearl. And in God's eyes, even compared to streets of gold and pearl gates, your wife is of great value. She is, after all, God's own daughter!

Men, that means as far as you are concerned, you can't even describe how valuable she should be to you. That's why Peter goes on to say, "Likewise, you husbands, dwell with them according to knowledge, giving honor unto the wife as unto the weaker vessel" (v. 7).

Let me deal with something real quick, and then I'll come back to that. She is not the weaker vessel. I believe we established that in chapter one and two. She is strong and capable. You're doing good just to keep up with her. But you are supposed to honor her *as if* she were a weaker vessel.

Giving her *honor* means "to value as extremely costly and extremely pricey." Why? He goes on to say, "as being heirs together of the grace of life; that your prayers be not hindered." You have been given a gift that God sees as extremely valuable and costly. If you take that gift and treat it with little to no value, how do you expect your prayers to be fully active, powerful, or effective? You can't. Just as we saw in studying the foundations of your home, you must sit down *together* so that your prayers be not hindered.

Husbands, wives, heirs together in the grace of life, realize who the diamond in your household of faith is. Take a moment to acknowledge exactly how valuable and of great price she truly is in your life.

CHAPTER 6

TAKING IT TO THE NEW TESTAMENT

We have looked at a lot of scriptures, definitions, and principles in the Old Testament, but do these truths carry over into the New Testament? We've seen in the Old Testament how the wife should build the house. Now let's look in the New Testament how the Master Builder builds His house!

John 7:16 says, "Jesus answered them, and said, My doctrine is not mine, but his that sent me." Also look at John 12:49–50, "For I have not spoken of myself; but the Father which sent me, he gave me a commandment, what I should say, and what I should speak. And I know that his commandment is life everlasting: whatsoever I speak therefore, even as the Father said unto me, so I speak." The *Weymouth Translation* says, "I speak just as the Father has bidden me." Let's read one more scripture in John 14:10, "Believest thou not that I am in the Father, and the Father in me? The words that I speak unto you I speak not of myself: but the Father that dwelleth in me, he doeth the works."

Let me make those scriptures a little more concise and give you the Weeter translation: "I speak the Father's words and He does the works." The Chief Cornerstone of the household—Jesus—used the Father's words to build the Church—the house of God.

The following passage in Ephesians brings us full circle back to the concept of the foundation of the household. "Now therefore ye are no more strangers and foreigners, but fellow citizens with the saints, and of the household of God; And are built upon the *foundation* of the apostles and prophets, Jesus Christ himself being the *chief corner stone;* In Whom all the building fitly framed together groweth unto a holy temple in the Lord: in whom ye also are builder together for a habitation of God through the Spirit" (Ephesians 2:19–22, italics added).

This is the Master Builder's pattern—His blueprint. It's how Jesus operated, and also how the diamond should operate. The diamond speaks the Father's words then the Father does the work of laying the foundations of home through her and then her labor is not in vain.

Chapter Six: Taking it to the New Testament

Another meaning of the word *foundation* in Ephesians 5 and Isaiah 54 is to teach or to instruct. Jesus went about teaching as part of His process in building the House of the Lord. Satan has been able to rob the households of faith and the Church by keeping the woman of the house from being able to teach. Through religious tradition, there's been great and gross misunderstanding, therefore a significant shift in mindset needs to take place concerning this topic in the Church at large.

Beginning in 1 Corinthians 14:33, "For God is not the author of confusion, but of peace, as in all churches of the saints." We should not be confused on these issues, instead we should have peace about them. So let's continue in these verses, "Let your women keep silence in the churches." The same Greek word translated as "women" also means "wives."

With that in mind, continue reading, "For it is not permitted unto them to speak; but they are commanded to be under obedience as also saith the law. And if they will learn any thing, let them ask their husbands at home: for it is a shame for women to speak in the church."

In the second half of this verse, it mentions husbands. Now the woman has to be a wife in order to ask her husband, right? Contextually this is speaking of a husband/wife relationship.

Let's go immediately over to 1 Timothy 2:11, "Let the woman learn in silence with all subjection. But I suffer not a woman to teach, or to usurp authority over the man, but to be in silence."

In some Christian denominations, women have not been allowed—they have even been forbidden—to teach, preach, or in some cases audibly pray in church based on these two scriptures. Even more demonic than that, this mindset of inequality, inferiority, and incompetence has carried over into the home and families of the household of faith. As Brother Kenneth E. Hagin used to say, "Bless their darlin' hearts and stupid heads." That is ignorance gone to seed! It's ignorance because those who perpetuate this belief didn't take the time to stop, study, and research what the words meant.

Those who have taught this incorrect doctrine didn't rightly discern the scriptures. Was it talking about women? Was it talking about wives? Was it talking

Chapter Six: Taking it to the New Testament

about a particular church situation that was going on inside a particular culture? Was it supposed to apply to all churches for all time in every situation?

While the focus of this book is specifically the wife being the diamond in the household of faith, Brother Kenneth E. Hagin wrote a book called *The Woman Question*. In it, he addresses in detail these scriptures as they apply to the woman's place in the church. Should she preach in the church? Should she teach in the church? Should she hold positions of authority in the church? How did all of these scriptures apply to the operation of the church itself and its function and leadership? I encourage you to read his book on the subject.

In *The Woman Question,* Brother Hagin references the Law of Scriptural Interpretation which is this: "Every scripture must be interpreted in the light of what other scriptures have to say on the same subject. It must harmonize with all other scripture."[4] Much error has resulted in ignoring this law of interpretation. Anyone can lift verses out of their settings, ignore the law of interpretation, and make them say anything

4 Hagin, Kenneth E. The Woman Question. Faith Library Publications, 1983.

you want them to say about anything. This is what has happened with these two particular scriptures in 1 Corinthians 14 and 1 Timothy 2.

Let me show you other scriptures throughout the Bible that clearly support the fact that these have been grossly misinterpreted and incorrectly discerned causing much confusion instead of peace in the Church.

Our foundation scriptures for this study are Proverbs 31 and Isaiah 54. So let's look at them once again. In talking about the virtuous woman in Proverbs 31, it actually says in verse 26, "She openeth her mouth with wisdom." In the *Strong's Concordance,* it shows that she speaks and teaches wisdom! Just in this one verse we see that the very nature of a virtuous woman includes the idea of instructing, not only speaking but also teaching.

Remember, in Isaiah 54 we saw part of the meaning of the word foundation is to teach and instruct. Indeed, verse 13 says, "And all your children shall be taught of the Lord." He's the Master Builder but He builds the home *through* the diamond. He does the teaching through her.

Chapter Six: Taking it to the New Testament

Proverbs 19:14 reads, "House and riches are the inheritance of fathers: and a prudent wife is from the Lord." As you'll remember, prudent includes the meaning "to instruct." A prudent wife is to instruct!

This next passage in 2 Timothy 1:5 is quite fascinating to me because of Timothy's heritage. This book is a letter from Paul to his spiritual son, Timothy. Paul writes, "When I call to remembrance the unfeigned faith that is in you, which dwelt first in your grandmother Lois, and your mother Eunice; and I am persuaded that in you also." Notice it doesn't say anything about Grandpa or Dad. It dwelt first in the grandmother then in the mother.

Faith comes by hearing the spoken Word of God, and Timothy heard it from his grandmother and from his mother!

How does faith come? Faith comes by hearing and hearing by the Word of God. (See Romans 10:17.) That word "Word" is specifically the spoken word—*rhema* in the Greek. Faith comes by hearing the spoken Word of God, and Timothy heard it from his grandmother and from his mother! They taught him faith.

They spoke the Word to him and faith took root. It was unfeigned, pure faith from his mother and grandmother's teaching of the Word.

Titus was another spiritual son of Paul's. In Titus 2, Paul wrote specific instructions, "But speak thou the things which become sound doctrine: That the aged men be sober, grave, temperate, sound in faith, in charity, in patience. The aged women likewise, that they be in behaviour as becometh holiness, not false accusers, not given to much wine, *teachers* of good things; That they may teach the young women to be sober, to love their husbands, to love their children" (vv. 1–4, italics added). They teach! Scripture after scripture says that women are supposed to teach.

Some could argue that those examples show women teaching only in their home, so let's keep digging.

"And there was one Anna, a prophetess…and she was a widow of about fourscore and four years, which departed not from *the temple,* but she served God with fastings and prayers night and day. And she coming in that instant gave thanks likewise unto the Lord, and *spake of him* to all them that looked for redemption in

Jerusalem" (Luke 2:36–38, italics added). Anna served God in the church speaking to all who were looking for redemption. A prophetess in the true sense of the word speaks the Word of the Lord.

They teach! Scripture after scripture says that women are supposed to teach.

Another instance of a woman speaking and teaching can be found in Acts. "And [Apollos] began to speak boldly in the synagogue: whom when Aquila *and Priscilla* had heard, *they* took him unto them, and expounded unto him the way of God more perfectly" (Acts 18:26, italics added). Priscilla alongside her husband taught and expounded the way of God to Apollos.

My purpose for this book is not to teach on women's roles in the church, however, we have clearly demonstrated through scripture that it is God-ordained for the diamond to teach and expound the things of God in the home and even outside of it. Indeed, as we saw in the word *foundation,* it is an integral part of her purpose.

I've noticed also a difference between Jewish women and the Gentiles whom Paul preached to. This cultural difference certainly factors in to the scriptures that we looked at in 1 Corinthians and in 2 Timothy talking about women keeping silent in the church. With research you'll find that the women in the Greek and Roman cultures were kept quite ignorant. Some Bible commentaries speak of the fact that women would blurt things out in the middle of the church service having nothing to do with the service whatsoever. Paul was writing these letters to the church of Corinth and to Timothy in order to address this disruptive behavior.

However, every instance we have looked at in Scripture where the women were teaching and speaking the Word of the Lord, including the prophetess Anna and Timothy's mother and grandmother, are examples of Jewish women. The Jews did not keep their women ignorant. They were well taught in the scriptures. Deborah in Judges 4 was a prophetess as well as a judge. She was a leader of the whole Jewish nation, obviously well-learned, as were all Jewish women.

There is a distinct difference in the cultures and the circumstances. The specific instructions Paul was giving to the church of Corinth in 1 Corinthians and what he was teaching in Timothy were a result of those particular women needing to be quiet during the church service. In fact, 1 Corinthians 14:34 where the *King James Version* says "women keep silent" is not an accurate translation. The word translated *women* is the Greek word *gune;* however, it can also be translated *wives*. With that in mind, Paul wrote 1 Corinthians 14:34 to say, "let your *[gune]* keep silent." But considering the very next verse says, "if they will learn anything, let them ask their husband's at home." Obviously, he was speaking about the wives who were being disruptive.

These verses were isolated cases dealing with specific situations in specific churches about a group and culture of people whose particular female segment was unlearned. Paul was instructing the most organized and systematic way to get rid of that inequality and bring the women up in their learning to the place where they were functioning equally in the church.

In essence, Paul was saying, "We need to get these women on the same level even though society has kept them ignorant and unlearned. Teach them at home, men. We don't need to be interrupting the whole church service to do this because we've got business to take care of, but be teaching them at home so there is equality and equal level of learning. Then they can be an integral part of the church."

Don't get me wrong here, the Gentile men were as scripturally unlearned as the women, seeing that they were not Jewish people. However, they had been instructed in intellectual and societal things. This was Paul's systematical and organized approach to achieve equality.

Why do I bring these things up? Because 1 Peter 3:7 talks to husbands. That's us, guys. The first thing he says is, "Likewise, you husbands, dwell with them according to knowledge." If the

> *Husbands and wives are meant to dwell together according to knowledge, and we've now obtained more knowledge about how to treat and honor the wife.*

husbands are going to dwell with the wives according to knowledge, then we have to know what we're talking about. We have to know what the wife is called to do. We have to know what her abilities and strengths are. We have to know what she is ordained by God to do. Now we have more knowledge! We know they're ordained to teach. They're ordained to speak the Word. They're ordained to walk in power, laying the foundations of the home.

Husbands and wives are meant to dwell together according to knowledge, and we've now obtained more knowledge about how to treat and honor the wife. "Giving honor unto the wife, as unto the weaker vessel, and as being heirs together of the grace of life." We are not heirs alone but co-heirs together. "That your prayers be not hindered" (1 Peter 3:7). In order to have a strong household, you must have a strong prayer life. "Having compassion one of another…be courteous…knowing that you are thereunto called, that ye should inherit a blessing" (vv. 8–9). All these things apply to the brethren, but because you are co-heirs, they apply to the wife as well.

CHAPTER 7

SUBMISSION

We've been skirting all around the issue of wives submitting to and obeying their husbands, and I'm not too good at skirting. I have a tendency to deal with things head on. In the last chapter, we discovered the Law of Scriptural Interpretation and the fact that you have to interpret scripture in light of scripture. I like what Brother Keith Moore said, "Do you know what you have to have to be scriptural? You have to have scripture!" It doesn't get a whole lot more simple than that. You have to have scripture to be scriptural!

Which do you think the Bible talks about more: wives submitting to their husbands or submitting one to another in the body of Christ in general? Often scripture will use terms like preferring another over yourself or loving your neighbor. Those verses far outnumber the "wives submit to your husbands" scriptures.

Submission and obedience is woven throughout the Bible for the entire body of Christ. However, that does not negate the fact that it is thoroughly scriptural that wives are to obey and submit to their own husbands. But what does that actually mean?

Remember, 1 Corinthians where Paul says, "Let your women keep silence in the churches." We discovered in the last chapter that the word *women* can also be translated "wives." "Let your *wives* keep silence in the churches: for it is not permitted unto them to speak; but they are commanded to be under obedience as also saith the law. And if they will learn any thing, let them ask their husbands at home: for it is a shame for women to speak in the church" (1 Corinthians 14:34–35, italics added).

Paul writes using the *same* word that can be translated wives in 1 Timothy 2, "Let the wives learn in silence with all subjection. But I suffer not a wife to teach, nor to usurp authority over the man." In the same way, that word *man* is translated *husband* as well. So we can accurately read, "But I suffer not a wife to teach, nor to usurp authority over her husband, but to be in silence." The subject being addressed is specifically a wife/husband relationship, not a woman/man relationship.

With that reiterated and settled, let's read Ephesians 5:21, "Submitting yourselves one to another in the fear of God." Then Paul breaks the idea of submission down further over the next 11 verses, beginning with verse 22, "Wives, submit yourselves unto your own husbands, as unto the Lord."

What does it actually mean to submit? The word *submit* comes from the Greek word *hupotasso,* meaning "to subordinate, to obey, to be under obedience, put under, subdue unto, be subject to, and in subjection to." This is a combination of two root words: *hupo* and *tasso.* The root word *hupo* means "to be under, to be beneath, or to be lower than." The word *tasso* means "to arrange in an orderly manner, to assign or dispose, to determine, appoint or ordain, to set in an orderly manner."

So the intent of wives submitting themselves to their own husbands is to establish order and a chain of command. Paul lays out the order quite clearly: Christ is the head of man, God is the head of Christ. It's a chain of command. Submit means to be under, and the word *obey* literally means "to obey." It means "to hear as a subordinate, to heed or conform to a command or authority."

So this is in scripture. It's not a figment of religious imagination.

Stay with me though. Some things have a tendency to get overlooked. Notice it says, "Wives, submit *yourselves* unto your own husbands." First of all, the wife is to submit to her own husband, not to any other man. Secondly, this verse is addressed specifically to the wives and says to submit *yourselves*. Husbands, it does *not* say, "Husbands make your wives submit to you." Neither does Christ make us submit to him. This is an act of the wife's own will.

Next, let's examine the phrase "as unto the Lord." I like the way Paul states it in Colossians 3:18, "Wives, submit yourselves unto your own husbands, as it is fit in the Lord."

Brother Kenneth E. Hagin told a story of a minister demanding that his wife had to submit to him without question. If he told her to sleep with another man, then she had to sleep with another man, because she was to obey unquestioningly. Wrong! That is a lie!

Wives are to submit "as unto the Lord" and "as it is fit in the Lord." Adultery, lying, stealing, and any other thing that does not line up with scripture is not "fit in the Lord."

Husbands, listen up! You better make sure that you are lined up with the Word if you expect your wife to submit to you and what you say. All bets are off if it does not line up with the Word!

❖ Our Biblical Chain of Command ❖

Let's revisit the chain of command concept that goes along with the word "submit." First Corinthians 11:3 says, "But I would have you know, that the head of every man is Christ; and the head of the woman is the man." Now again, we have the same translation situation and this can be translated *wife* and *husband*. God is the head of Christ who is the head of the husband who is the head of the wife. So here we have the chain of command within the structure of the family unit as designed by God.

This flow of authority is not because one is subordinate to another in equality, ability, or anointing.

Jesus is not subordinate to God yet God is His head. Same goes for the wife and the husband.

Most people don't think of Jesus submitting Himself to God. So let's look at this in scripture. Jesus is talking in John 5:30, "I can of mine own self do nothing: as I hear, I judge: and my judgment is just; because I seek not mine own will, but the will of the Father which hath sent me." Jesus is not seeking His own will but His Father's. He is placing His will under subjection to His Father's will.

If John 5 wasn't clear enough, let's read Luke 22. Jesus was in the garden of Gethsemane when He said, "Father, if thou be willing, remove this cup from me: nevertheless not my will, but thine, be done" (v. 42). What a beautiful picture of complete submission and obedience by Jesus to His head, the Father. He was about to undergo horrendous torture, physical and spiritual death, but He (of His own choosing and His own will) submitted Himself to His spiritual head, His Father.

Philippians 2:5 tell us the way Jesus thought and how He conducted His life. "Let this mind be in you, which was also in Christ Jesus. Who, being in the form of God, thought it not robbery to be equal with God." So, He is in equal standing with God, but look at what it says next, "But made himself of no reputation, and took upon him the form of a servant, and was made in the likeness of men: And being found in fashion as a man, he humbled himself, and became obedient unto death, even the death of the cross." Did you see that? Even though He was in the form of God and He was equal to God, Jesus—of His own free will— submitted Himself to the will of God, humbled Himself, and took the form of a servant, who is literally below or submitted in obedience to someone else. That sounds a lot like "submit yourselves."

Although I didn't include these descriptions previously—I didn't want you to burn the book until I could explain it in more detail—two of the descriptions included in the words translated *submission* are "slave and servant." In 1 Peter 3 and Ephesians 5, that word *servant* is contained in the definitions of those words *submit* and *obey* as well. So we can see that this is exactly how Jesus operated in relation to His head, the Father

God. What a beautiful example! That's one reason the Holy Spirit had Paul explain the chain of command in this manner: the head of Christ is God, the head of man is Christ, the head of the wife is the husband. It demonstrates the chain of command in the earth.

◆ Head of the House ◆

Even though it is a common term, nowhere in the Bible does it say that the man is the head of the house. It says he is the head of his wife. Not only is there no instruction in the Bible for the husband to be the head of the household, the opposite is actually true! Paul, in giving instruction to his spiritual son Timothy regarding how things should be conducted in the church, told him that it was young women who should be the heads and rulers of the family! "I will therefore that the younger women marry, bear children, guide the house, give none occasion to the adversary to speak reproachfully" (1 Timothy 5:14).

According to *Strong's Concordance,* the Greek word that is translated as "guide the house" is *oikodespoteo* and literally means "to be the head of (i.e. rule) a family."

This is supported by the authority structure we just saw laid out by God through Paul. God is the head of Christ, Christ is the head of the man, the husband is the head of the wife, the wife is the head of the house. When Jesus was raised from the dead and God raised Him up to be the head of the Church, He turned around and gave us all of His authority to rule the earth and have dominion over it, bringing it into subjection to the Word. Husbands, as the heads of their wives, should be giving their wives complete authority and power to rule the household and bring it into subjection to the Word of God!

❖ Even as Sarah... ❖

We have looked at 1 Peter 3 a couple of times, but we skipped over something important. Every time we go back, we gain more knowledge which is exactly what 1 Peter talks about: "to dwell with them according to knowledge." We see things in a different light when we have more knowledge.

So let's reread 1 Peter 3:5–6, "For after this manner in the old time the holy women also, who trusted in

God, adorned themselves, being in subjection unto their own husbands: Even as Sarah..." Alright, let's look at Sarah.

Her story is found in Genesis 16:1, "Now Sarai, Abram's wife bare him no children: and she had a handmaid, an Egyptian, whose name was Hagar. So Sarai said unto Abram, Behold now, the Lord hath restrained me from bearing. I pray thee, go in unto my maid; it may be that I may obtain children by her. And Abram hearkened to the voice of Sarai. And Sarai Abram's wife took Hagar her maid the Egyptian, after Abram had dwelt ten years in the land of Canaan, and gave her to her husband Abram to be his wife. And he went in unto Hagar, and she conceived: and when she saw that she had conceived, her mistress was despised in her eyes."

Sarah made a mistake. First of all, she mistakenly placed the blame on God for "restraining her from bearing." But also, she didn't walk in faith. She didn't stand on what the Lord had promised. Instead she tried to help the Lord out and make the prophecy come true. In doing so, she made a very big mistake.

She said to Abram, "My wrong be upon you" (v. 5). In other words, "That's what you get for being my head!"

"Sarai said unto Abram, My wrong be upon thee: I have given my maid into thy bosom; and when she saw that she had conceived, I was despised in her eyes: the Lord judge between me and thee. But Abram said unto Sarai, Behold, thy maid is in thine hand; do to her as it pleases you. And when Sarai dealt hardly with her, she fled from her face."

Throughout chapters 16–21, there was strife between Sarah, her maid, and Abraham. Then they added kids in the mix. What a mess! The exciting conclusion takes place in Genesis 21:10–12, "Wherefore she said unto Abraham, Cast out this bondwoman and her son: for the son of this bondwoman shall not be heir with my son, even with Isaac. And the thing was very grievous in Abraham's sight because of his son. And God said unto Abraham, Let it not be grievous in your sight because of the lad, and because of the bondwoman; in all that Sarah hath said unto you, hearken unto her voice; for in Isaac shall thy seed be called."

Here's the synopsis: Sarah made a demand. Abraham disagreed and it grieved him, but he did what she asked. God backed Sarah.

It looks to me like Sarah had plenty of authority in the house. She was not blindly submissive. Even though she made the original mistake, she went to Abraham and asked him to step in and fix it. She stood her ground knowing that it was God's perfect plan for the promise to come through Isaac.

💎 Women of Faith 💎

Sarah is used as an example in 1 Peter 3 as a holy woman who trusted in God. What does that description mean? These women had faith! They walked in faith and trusted in God.

These women also "adorned themselves, being in subjection unto their own husbands." So they dressed to please their own husbands.

They obeyed their husbands as unto the Lord, as it was fit in the Lord, and they had extreme reverence. "Even as Sarah obeyed Abraham, calling him lord." The word lord is actually used like a surname and can also mean master or sir. So yes, ladies, you are to have extreme reverence for your husbands. That is how the Lord set it up.

But what if your husband isn't worthy of reverence? Remember these were women of faith. Sometimes they had to call things that be not as though they were. So, if your husband doesn't seem worthy, act like God and call things that be not as though they are. Treat him like he deserves the extreme reverence that you give him.

Notice, too, the women here were not afraid. Sarah was not scared of Abraham. She did not call him *lord* out of fear. We know this because the verse goes on to say they "are not afraid with any amazement." They were not "chicken women!" Faith and fear can't dwell together. These were women of faith who trusted God, so they were not afraid of their husbands. Sarah stood up to Abraham when she needed to stand up and called him out on things that weren't right. She wasn't afraid of him. She had deep reverence and respect for her husband.

> *They obeyed their husbands as unto the Lord, as it was fit in the Lord, and they had extreme reverence.*

It is no problem submitting to someone you respect, just as Jesus submitted to God because of the reverence and honor He gave. That is how God set it up. Not only for the wife to submit, but for the husband to be worthy of her submission by lining up with the Word of God.

CHAPTER 8
TO THE HUSBANDS

A lot of times men seem to forget that there are a greater number of verses in Ephesians 5 talking about the men's responsibility in loving their wives than there are about wives submitting to their husbands. Only 3 verses specifically talk about the wives. Men, we've got 10 verses dealing with the husband's responsibility!

We are to love and treat our wives as Christ loves and treats the Church. That is a foundational principle for husbands to understand.

So how does Jesus love and treat the Church? "Let this mind be in you, which was also in Christ Jesus: Who, being in the form of God, thought it not robbery to be equal with God" (Philippians 2:5). The Son submitted to God the Father. He "made himself of no reputation, and took upon him the form of a servant, and was made in the likeness of men: And being found in fashion as a man, he humbled himself." He submitted Himself by becoming "obedient unto death, even the death of the cross" (vv. 7–8).

As an act of His will, Jesus submitted Himself unto His God. These verses demonstrate what we saw Jesus saying in the last chapter. "If there's any way, let this cup pass nevertheless not my will, but your will." (See Luke 22:42.) He submitted to the will of His Head.

But look what His Head did when Jesus submitted: "Wherefore God also hath highly exalted him, and given him a name which is above every name" (Philippians 2:9).

Compare that to what we already saw in 1 Corinthians 11. God is the head of Christ; Christ is the head of man; the husband is the head of the wife. So Jesus submitted Himself to God; God raised Him up and gave Him His name. In the same way, when the wife submits herself to the husband, what should the husband do? That's right, raise her up and give her his name. Do you see the parallel? She submits herself of her own free will to her head, and her head turns around and raises her up and says, "Yes, you are equal in this household."

Keep that principle firmly in your mind as we continue.

❖ The Blessing ❖

We saw how God related to Jesus when Jesus submitted Himself to His head. Now, let's look at some examples how Jesus, the Head of the Church, relates to the Church, because that's how the husband is supposed to relate to his wife.

Hebrews 7:24 is talking about Jesus when Paul says, "But this man because he continueth ever, hath an unchangeable priesthood. Wherefore he is able also to save them to the uttermost that come unto God by him, seeing he ever liveth to make intercession for them." That is what Jesus is doing right now for the Church! He ever liveth to make intercession for us.

The vast majority of the Church who reads the following passage doesn't understand the importance and the significance of it. But you are about to! Look at Luke 24:50, "And he [Jesus] led them out as far as to Bethany, and he lifted up his hands, and blessed them. And it came to pass, while he blessed them, he was parted from them, and carried up into heaven." He was not waiting around for them to sneeze and then said, "Oh God bless you." That is not what this is talking about. He is forever our High Priest after the order of Melchizedek. It is His job and responsibility to declare and pronounce the blessing on the Church. And it was so important to Him that He raised His hands and as He blessed them, the power of the blessing He was pronouncing raised Him up and He was carried up into heaven declaring the blessing on them.

If this is the first time you've ever heard that, it may be a little strange to you. As I show you what the blessing is, we will plant a seed that will produce a tremendous harvest in your life. If you have heard it before, then we will water the seed and build your faith.

To be clear, this is not a blessing but *the* blessing! A blessing might be a car, for example, but *the blessing* is the spiritual force released by God that produces the car.

Before we look at exactly what the blessing is, however, I want to point something out to you. I am not just picking out something that Jesus did for the Church and saying, "Hey, we ought to do this as husbands to our wives just as Christ does to us." This specific example I'm using because it goes line-upon-line, precept-upon-precept, hand-in-hand with one of the few instructions to husbands contained within our foundation scripture of Proverbs 31.

Almost the entire chapter of Proverbs 31 is about the virtuous woman managing her household. There is almost nothing describing what the husband does except trust in her. He sits and visits with the elders at the gates (v. 23), and "her children rise up and call her blessed. Her husband also and he praises her" (v. 28). One of the things that the husband is supposed to do is call his wife blessed. He should be pronouncing and declaring the blessing over her, just as we saw Jesus do with the Church in Luke 24.

To tell the truth, we could write entire books on what it means to bless someone, what the blessing is and what it does. In fact, people have. I encourage you to study the topic of the blessing out further because this is essential for husbands in knowing how we are supposed to treat our wives. There are excellent books out there on the blessing. Brother Kenneth Copeland has one called *The Blessing of the Lord: It Maketh Rich and He Adds No Sorrow With It*. I highly recommend this book! Read it. Study it. Research it. Find out what the blessing does because this is what you're supposed to be declaring over your wife.

One of the things that the husband is supposed to do is call his wife blessed.

Remember, Jesus constantly makes intercession for us and blesses us. Therefore, you should constantly make intercession declaring the blessing over your wife. Let's break down what that means.

Starting at the beginning in Genesis 1, God had just finished creating the animals and the fish. Then He created man, but before He was finished He had one more thing to do. Verse 28 tells us the blessing God gave, "And God blessed them and God said unto them, Be fruitful, and multiply, and replenish the earth, and subdue it: and have dominion over the fish of the sea, and over the fowl of the air, and over every living thing that moves upon the earth." That is the blessing of God!

Up until that time, God looked at what He created and said "it was good" (vv. 4, 10, 12, 18, 21, 25), but after man was created and the blessing given, He called it "very good" (v. 31).

We see the blessing over and over throughout scripture. In Genesis 9, mankind had come to the point where God had to start over again. So, after the flood, the only living people on the planet were Noah and his family. What did He do? "And God blessed Noah and his sons, and said unto them, Be fruitful, and multiply, and replenish the earth. And the fear of you and the dread of you shall be upon every beast of the earth, and upon every fowl of the air, upon all that moveth upon the earth, and upon all the fishes of the sea; into your hand are they delivered" (vv. 1–2). God reestablished the blessing in the earth and released the blessing into Noah and his family.

Again in Genesis 12:1–3, "Now the Lord had said unto Abram get thee out of thy country, and from thy kindred, and from thy father's house, unto a land that I will shew thee: And I will make of thee a great nation, and I will bless you, and make your name great; and you shalt be a blessing: And I will bless them that bless thee, and curse him that curseth thee: and in thee shall all families of the earth be blessed." You can trace the blessing all through scripture to see God's plan. In Genesis 17:6, "And I will make thee exceeding fruitful, and I will make nations of thee, and kings shall come out of thee. And I will establish my covenant between me and thee and thy seed." Did you notice that right there in verse 6? "I will make thee exceeding fruitful." Sound familiar? It's repeated again in chapters 26 and 28.

The blessing doesn't stop in the Old Testament. No! In Galatians 3:13 it tells us, "Christ hath redeemed us from the curse of the law, being made a curse for us: for it is written, Cursed is every one that hangeth on a tree: That the blessing of Abraham might come on the Gentiles through Jesus Christ; that we might receive the promise of the Spirit through faith." He tells us plainly that the whole reason Jesus came to earth was to get the blessing back to people, now He ever lives to declare and pronounce that blessing over the Church!

Are you declaring the blessing over your wife? Are you purposely releasing your faith into words of blessing over her to raise her up into a position of authority and dominion over your home and over your household, under your prayer and praise? Are you ever living to do that? That's what God did for Jesus and for us.

Keep in mind our comparison between Christ and man, and the husband and wife as you read the next couple verses. Ephesians 1:22–23 says that God "hath put all things under [Jesus] feet, and gave him to be *the head* over all things to the church, Which is his body" (italics added). Also, in chapter 2:6, God "hath raised us up together, and made us sit together in heavenly places in Christ Jesus."

Jesus submitted Himself to God. Then what did God do? As His head, He turned around and exalted Him, gave Him a name which is above every name, raised Him up to sit with Him in heavenly places. We submit ourselves to Christ, and God raises us up together with Christ, seats us with Him and His authority in heavenly places. This joint heirship with

Jesus (see Romans 8:17) is one of the primary factors needed so "that your prayers be not hindered" (1 Peter 3:7). Jesus submitted Himself to God; God exalted Him. We submit ourselves to Christ; we've been raised up together with Christ and seated with Him.

As the head of our wives, we husbands are to turn around and raise them up in the household, with equal authority as joint-heirs together in this life!

❖ Praise Her ❖

Now gentlemen, I would like to spend a little time on one small word from our foundational scripture of Proverbs 31. "Her children arise up, and call her blessed; her husband also, and he praiseth her" (v. 28). That word praise may be little, but my, oh my, does it hold so much meaning.

Along with declaring the blessing over her, we are to praise our wives. No sir, that does not mean that you say, "Good job, honey," once every six months or so. That's not going to cut it, guys!

The word *praise* contains the meaning "to be clear." You should make it clear to her how much she means to you and how valuable she is to you. Make it clear to everyone around. It means "to shine." (Perhaps like a diamond?!) You are to make it clear that she shines in your life and in your home. It also means "to make a show." Not only praise that she shines, but it's your job to polish that diamond, to make her shine like a show piece. Draw the luster and brilliance out of her.

Ladies, I know there's a stigma with the term "trophy wife" and the objectification of women. But there's a different aspect of that concept that is valid and biblical. Your husband wants to show you off, boast about you, brag on you, show off the shining diamond in his life.

Guys, it also means "to be clamorously foolish." You should be a fool for your wife's love. Act a fool for her! Celebrate your diamond! Celebrate your virtuous wife. Sing her praises. Okay, for some of us, our literal singing may not be a wonderful sound, but sing the praises of your diamond. All of those concepts are contained in that one small word *praiseth*. Not only are you to praise God. You are to praise your virtuous wife.

💎 Nourish Her 💎

Most people see 1 Corinthians 7:1–5, as only describing the sexual relationship between a husband and a wife. It is clearly dealing with that subject. But I want to put a new perspective on it as well. "Now concerning the things whereof ye wrote unto me: It is good for a man not to touch a woman. Nevertheless, to avoid fornication, let every man have his own wife, and let every woman have her own husband." Again, we see the words man and woman could also be translated husband and wife. And yes, the word *have* is possessive on both parts.

"Let the husband render unto the wife due benevolence," meaning "conjugal duties." Notice it is his responsibility listed first.

"And likewise also the wife unto the husband. The wife hath not power of her own body, but the husband: and likewise also the husband has not power of his own body, but the wife. Defraud you not one the other, except it be with consent for a time, that you may give yourselves to fasting and prayer; and come together again, that Satan tempt you not for your

Chapter Eight: To the Husbands

incontinency." Clearly this is dealing with the sexual relationship between a husband and wife. But I want to go back up and point out verse 4, "The wife has not power of her own body." Power also means authority. The husband has the right and authority to pray for his wife's healing, physical protection, and deliverance on a level that no one else has.

> *The husband has the right and authority to pray for his wife's healing, physical protection, and deliverance on a level that no one else has.*

Not too long after Lynn and I had gotten married that we were at a friend's house and spent most of the day there. Toward evening, Lynn became extremely sick. In a matter of minutes, she became delirious and was at the point of passing out. I prayed earnestly over her and heard in my spirit the first line of Psalm 23, "The Lord is my Shepard, I shall not want."

I leaned over and whispered it in her ear as she was slumped against the wall.

She told me later that when she first heard that line, it sounded far off in the distance but then it was like the rest of Psalm 23 exploded in her entire being so loudly that it was all consuming.

Within a matter of fifteen or twenty minutes, she was entirely whole and thinking clearly just as if nothing happened!

I prayed and interceded as the head of my wife and the Lord gave me His Words. They came through me into her to save, heal, and deliver her body over which I had authority! That's a picture of how this system works.

Look back at Ephesians 5:23, "For the husband is the head of the wife, even as Christ is the head of the church: and he is the savior of the body." That word *savior* is actually the same word that's used throughout scripture to describe Jesus as our Savior, and the root word, *sozo,* is the same used as *salvation* in Romans 10:10, "With the heart man believeth unto righteousness and with the mouth confession is made unto salvation." It means protection, deliverance, safety, health, and healing. These are the things that the husband is to be for his wife.

Please don't misunderstand me at all. I'm not saying that the husband is the wife's savior. A wife cannot be born again through her husband. That is not true. He is not the savior of her spirit. He has authority over her body. He has more power and authority than anyone else to pray for her healing, protection, deliverance, etc.

Ephesians 5 goes on to explain in verse 29, "For no man ever yet hated his own flesh; but nourisheth and cherisheth it, even as the Lord the church." The word *nourish* means "to bring up, to build up, to raise up." That's what the husband is supposed to do for his wife. He builds her up and raises her. And he does so through declaring the blessing over her and ever living to intercede praises on her behalf.

❦ Be the Anchor ❦

Before we leave Ephesians 5 completely, there is one more thing I want to point out. It has to do with the Greek word and definition of the English word *head* used in verse 23. This word literally means "something to be seized upon." In other words, the head is an anchor and stabilizer. This particular meaning is a source of humor in our home and has a profound undertone for my wife specifically.

My wife has become skilled over time through training with various elite, tactical units around the world. She is vastly more qualified than most men in protecting and defending her home and those she loves! Seeing that I do a tremendous amount of traveling with the ministry, this has always been a distinct advantage in our home.

> *In other words, the head is an anchor and stabilizer.*

Once when my son, Ryan, was about 5 years old, I was out of town and the kids got to sleep in my place in the bed which was something they looked forward to with great joy! One night in the early hours of the morning, there was a loud noise that woke both my wife and my son up, which was significant in Ryan's case! They both recognized the noise as someone trying to gain entrance to our home.

So Lynn instructed Ryan where to hide for safety. She took possession of her firearm and proceeded to "clear" the house.

Chapter Eight: To the Husbands

This being done, she returned to the bedroom where our son was ready with a question. "Mom, what would you have done if someone had broken into our home?"

Lynn said, "No one is going to endanger my children, Ryan. I would have shot them."

Ryan continued, "Would you have just tried to wound them or something?"

"No, son, I would have killed them."

Ryan breathed a big sigh of relief, "Okay, good!" And he promptly went back to sleeping soundly again. He had the reassurance that he was well-protected by love.

I told you that story because it shows how confident my children were in Lynn's ability to protect them and the home. Yet anytime I return from a trip, they all immediately start yawning and getting sleepy! It is such a funny phenomenon. My wife laughs and says, "I know it seems funny to you, but we all feel so much more at peace and safe when you are home. You bring such stability and steadfastness to the family."

Then she expresses those sentiments in a little more intimate detail later in the evening!

This is what the husband is supposed to be: the anchor and the stabilizer for his wife.

💎 Specific to Your Wife 💎

Guys, make a practice of what is outlined in this chapter and ask the Holy Spirit to show you how to walk these things out in practical ways specifically for your wife. Every woman is different. You dwell with your wife according to knowledge, so you know her better than anyone. There are things that will mean more to her than they would to another woman. Be led by the spirit and walk these things out practically.

If you do, I can pretty much guarantee two things. Number one, she will not have any problem whatsoever submitting to you and your authority over her. Having the

> *Every woman is different. You dwell with your wife according to knowledge, so you know her better than anyone.*

type of respect and honor for you that Sarah of old did when she called Abraham "lord" or "master" will not be a problem because you've given her someone to respect. Number two, the subject matter being discussed in 1 Corinthians 7:1–5 will indeed be a wonderful and glorious part of your marriage.

CHAPTER 9
THE RICH WIFE

This study has perhaps killed a few sacred cows, so we might as well knock a few more right between the eyes. Maybe we can finally wipe out this whole devil-inspired herd of religious lies!

We have seen the wife's inherent value: Far more precious than rubies or pearls. This shows her immense value based on her personal qualities and who she is designed by God to be.

But there is another aspect of the diamond in the household of faith that is so interwoven in almost every description of her in scripture that it is part of her spiritual DNA. What does the Bible depict her as being in possession of? She is supposed to be financially wealthy and very rich in goods and material things. She is supposed to live in luxury and have luxurious things. And these riches and luxury are not all up to the husband.

We see the significance of this idea in our foundation passage of Proverbs 31 which lists many things about the wife that indicate wealth, riches, and luxury beginning with the first verse talking about her. Remember, the definition of *virtuous* includes "means and resources, goods, riches, and substance."

As a matter of fact, the virtuous woman travels and her family eats imported food (v. 14). "She rises while it is yet night and gets [spiritual] food for her household and assigns her maids their tasks" (v. 15, AMPC). Yes, she has maids and servants who are well taken care of and well-dressed (v. 21) to help her around the house, because as we read on, you'll see she's quite busy. She considers different fields, evaluates different plots of real estate, then buys the properties that make good business sense (v. 16). She has good, quality merchandise (v. 18) that she makes of fine linens and sells (v. 24). She is generous and has plenty to give to the needy (v. 20).

Sounds to me like God makes all grace abound toward her so that she has sufficiency in all things and is able to abound to every good work (2 Corinthians 9:8). She's not afraid of the winter or hard seasons because her whole household is well-clothed (v. 21), as is she with luxurious, expensive clothing of silk and purple (v. 22). Now this isn't to say that all wives should be wearing silk and purple. In the culture and climate of that day, those fabrics and colors were exceedingly expensive items. The point is she has great business sense, works hard, and takes care of herself. This woman is wealthy and prosperous!

We can reexamine the scripture, "Whoso findeth a wife findeth a good thing, and obtaineth favor of the Lord" (Proverbs 18:22) where the word *good* in its definition denotes "bountiful, prosperity, and wealth." Also in Proverbs 19:14 where it says "a prudent wife is from the Lord," the definition of *prudent* includes "to prosper and to have good success."

And we dare not overlook the financial worth of the very gemstones that she has throughout her home in Isaiah 54. Those are not just figurative gemstones. This is proven out in Psalm 112:3 as the Lord says that "wealth and riches are in [the righteous man's] house." You don't

> *The point is she has great business sense, works hard, and takes care of herself. This woman is wealthy and prosperous!*

think they got there all by themselves, do you? No, the diamond of the righteous man's household laid his foundations and in those foundations were wealth and riches!

Looking at definitions is one thing, but do we have any specific examples of godly women being wealthy in scripture? Why yes, as a matter of fact, we do! In the New Testament—which is our covenant—women supported Jesus' ministry with their wealth.

"And also a number of women who had been healed of many illnesses under his ministry and set free from demonic power. Jesus had cast out seven demons from one woman. Her name was Mary Magdalene... Among the women were Susanna and Joanna, the wife of Chusa, who managed King Herod's household. Many other women who supported Jesus' ministry from their own personal finances also traveled with him" (Luke 8:1–3 TPT). Another translation says they "used their considerable means to provide for the company" *(MSG)*.

These women gave of their considerable means to support Jesus's ministry and those who traveled with him! Notice it was *their* personal finances, not their husband's. It sure seems like these ladies were Proverbs 31 virtuous women.

Another example can be found in Acts 16:14, "And a certain woman named Lydia, a seller of purple…" Understand that in those days the seller of purple was almost equal in wealth to nobility because purple was so rare and expensive that only nobility was allowed to wear it. (That points right back to Proverbs 31 where the virtuous woman sells quality goods and clothes herself in silk and purple.) So as a seller of purple, Lydia was a very wealthy woman.

Let's keep reading, "And when she was baptized, and her household, she besought us, saying, If ye have judged me to be faithful to the Lord, come into my house, and live there. And she constrained us" (v. 15). In that culture and time, this meant she paid for *everything!* Moving in to the home of a man and woman as wealthy as nobility, Paul and his company lived quite well. Certainly not in a poor, poverty mentality the way some religious leaders have tried to teach. I'm sure Paul and his company were given only the best, because Lydia was a virtuous woman who was generous with her financial success.

The Word says out of the mouths of two or three witnesses let every word be established (Deut. 19:15). We have looked at more than two or three examples, and as we've read, God's plan for wives to be rich has been well established!

CHAPTER 10
THE WIFE—THE WARRIOR

We have explored many facets of the virtuous woman, but there is one more I want to dig into deeper. The virtuous woman is strong. She is submissive and equal to her husband. She is rich and prosperous. But now I want you to see that she is also a warrior.

The term virtuous woman is seen again in Proverbs 12:4 using the Hebrew word chayil. This word *chayil* describes a fierce warrior, but not only in this verse. *Chayil* is used throughout scripture, as we will see.

The angel of the Lord talks to Gideon in Judges 6:12, "The Lord is with thee, thou mighty man of valor." The word *valor* is the exact same Hebrew word *chayil* translated as virtuous in Proverbs 12:4 and Proverbs 31:10. The description of the mighty man of valor in Judges 6 is the same as the virtuous woman.

This man of valor or virtue is able to go in his might and save the entire nation of Israel (v. 14), and even wipe out the all the Midianites as one virtuous man (v. 16).

Again, in Joshua 1:14, God uses the same word as the virtuous woman to talk about the mighty men going into battle. "But you shall pass before your brethren armed, all the mighty men of valor and help them." Also, in 2 Chronicles 17:13,18: "The men of war, mighty men of valour, were in Jerusalem...prepared for the war." All through here the words *virtue* and *valor* are the same word.

No wonder Proverbs 12:4 continues to say, "A virtuous woman is a crown to her husband." The Lord used the word *virtuous* to describe women here because the Hebrew word for crown is *atarah* meaning "to encircle for attack or protection." Wow! This is why Proverbs 31:11–12,17 says, "The heart of her husband doth safely trust in her, so that he shall have no need of spoil. She will do him good and not evil all the days of her life….She girdeth her loins with strength, and strengtheneth her arms."

In other words, gentlemen, if you have a genuine diamond in her place in your household of faith who knows who she is, you don't need to worry about a thing. She will always have your back!

Chapter Ten: The Wife—The Warrior

One of our favorite movies is *Mr. and Mrs. Smith*. The main characters are a husband and wife, who were special agents in opposing agencies before they became married but didn't know it. They are both excellent in their field of tactile expertise. Their agencies find out they are married, and their new mission is to take each other out. But in the process, the Smiths discover that they are, in fact, truly in love. So, they decide to stand together as it should be. In the climatic scene of the movie, they face astronomical odds, out-numbered beyond belief, but they stand together. When the dust settles, the enemy is defeated and dead. And there Mr. and Mrs. Smith are, husband and wife, back-to-back, standing strong.

That is what the devil and every demon in hell should see when they even think about coming up against you, your family, or your household of faith. They literally don't stand a chance in hell of defeating you when the diamond in your household knows who she is and is in her place, *and* the husband trusts in her because he knows it as well.

CHAPTER 11

THE POWER OF TOGETHERNESS

To wrap this up, now that we've extensively studied these various passages and scriptures, I want to read these verses all together, keeping in mind the principles we've learned, and help solidify this picture in your mind. So look at the picture this paints:

> "Submitting yourselves one to another in the fear of God, let everyone of you in particular so love his wife even as himself, and the wife see that she reverences her husband. Nevertheless, neither is the man without the woman. Neither the woman without the man in the Lord. For as the woman is of the man, even so is the man also by the woman but all things of God. Let every man have his own wife, and let every woman have her own husband. Let the husband render unto the wife due benevolence and likewise also the wife unto the husband. The wife has not power over

her own body but the husband, and likewise also the husband has not power of his own body but the wife. Defraud you not one the other. There is neither Jew nor Greek, there is neither bond nor free, there is neither male nor female, for you are all one in Christ Jesus. And if you be Christ's, then are you Abraham's seed and heirs according to the promise. Marriage is honorable in all. It is valuable. Marriage is esteemed. Marriage is precious. Marriage is very pricey. And it should be held in esteem especially of the highest degree. And as being heirs together of the grace of life that your prayers be not hindered."

You can see through these scriptures the importance and stress placed on the power that the husband and wife have together. Not one dominating another. Not one nagging and complaining about the other. The power of togetherness is tremendous.

A number of years ago, Lynn began experiencing a multitude of physical symptoms including extreme fatigue, joint pain, sensitivity to noise and a lot of

Chapter Eleven: The Power of Togetherness

other miscellaneous and seemingly unrelated issues. Shortly after she began noticing them, she also began experiencing significant mental challenges. She wasn't able to complete sentences or think of even simple words like fork or shoe when she was trying to say them. She had extreme brain fog. Over the course of several years, it progressed to the point where if she came downstairs in the morning to vacuum the living room, she would have to stay in bed the rest of the day due to extreme exhaustion.

The power of togetherness is tremendous.

This type of thing is extremely rare around our home! Normally, if some physical issue arises, we pray while standing on our promises of healing contained in the Word and the issue disappears. So, needless to say, after several years of Lynn's health challenges getting worse, I sought the Lord and purposefully listened for the answer to this serious sickness.

There are a few things that are essential in these types of situations where a sickness drags on and prayer doesn't seem to be working. Among them are to never question if it's God's will for healing to take place; never entertain the idea that it might not be working; cast all the worry and care of the situation onto the Lord and then having done all to stand...keep standing. Keep listening for both spiritual instructions and natural, physical instructions.

I know that is easier said than done. When your wife is bed-bound for the day after brief activity and can't figure out how to say common words, it takes some diligence not to let your mind worry about the situation but it must be done!

But that is another teaching.

Anyway, we kept doing "business as usual" as much as she was physically able just as if she was healed and whole. In what seemed unrelated, someone asked us to research a set of symptoms that their wife was experiencing. Our background is in the medical field, so from time to time we are asked medical questions. I was busy with other things so I asked Lynn to research it for me.

Chapter Eleven: The Power of Togetherness

You have to remember that even through all of this I maintained my normal travel schedule and she kept the home running to the best of her ability including homeschooling our daughter! She had plenty of reasons to tell me no but she didn't. She took her place as my helpmate submitting herself to me as her head.

Well, I didn't realize it was anything miraculous. I didn't have any idea that the wisdom of God was about to be revealed! I was just praying and making supplication for my wife continually in the Spirit and doing what I was supposed to be doing. Lynn had no inclination that she was about to unlock the secret of what we had been searching for—for years at this point. She simply was doing what was right.

In the course of researching these other symptoms, she stumbled across an article about Lyme disease. She began researching the disease and discovered it included just about every symptom she had been suffering from for the last several years. In looking further into it, we found out that one of the leading Lyme disease specialists in the country lived in a town near us.

Lynn was tested and her results were positive for Lyme disease. Once we knew what it was, we pursued natural treatment but attacked it with the Word of God at the same time. She was pronounced completely free from that demonic disease in half the normal time! She is back to full function, healed and whole!

The answer came because I did what I was supposed to do, she did what she was supposed to do, and the Lord was able to get the answer to us and provide total deliverance! Thanks be to God Who *always* causes us to triumph in Him!

❖ One Body ❖

Let me remind you of what it says in Romans 12:4–8, "For as we have many members in one body, and all members have not the same office: So we, being many, are one body in Christ, and every one members one of another. Having then gifts differing according to the grace that is given to us, whether prophecy, let us prophesy according to the proportion of faith; Or ministry, let us wait on our ministering: or he that teacheth, on teaching." The gift of each member depends upon the anointing, grace, and calling.

This is the same pattern seen in Ephesians 4, "But unto every one of us is given grace according to the measure of the gift of Christ...But speaking the truth in love, may grow up into him in all things, which is the head even Christ: From whom the whole body fitly joined together and compacted by that which every joint supplies" (vv. 7,15). Remember Jesus told us, "Have ye not read, that he which made them at the beginning made them male and female...For this cause shall a man leave father and mother, and shall cleave to his wife: and they twain shall be one flesh? Wherefore they are no more twain, but one flesh. What therefore God hath joined together, let not man put asunder" (Matthew 19:4–6). The word translated *flesh* is literally *body*. Your marriage is a body—one body.

So, we see what happens as every joint is fitted together, but what happens if the joints are out of place in the body?

In writing this book, I spent a significant amount of time in prayer and meditation, and the Lord revealed something to me that I had never seen before. There was only one time in all of history when

Jesus' physical body was sick and diseased and that was when He was on the cross bearing sickness and disease for us! At that point in time, His body was so sick and diseased that it could no longer function properly—the point of death.

The prophet and psalmist, David, recorded the description of this physical death in Psalm 22. It was indeed prophetic of what Jesus Himself would say on the cross as He hung in excruciating physical pain and dysfunction. The psalm begins with "My God, my God, why have you forsaken me?" and ends with "it is finished" *(AMPC)*.

This prophetic psalm describes Jesus as his physical body was dying a severely painful death. "I am poured out like water, and all my bones are out of joint: my heart is like wax; it is melted in the midst of my bowels. My strength is dried up like a potsherd; and my tongue cleaveth to my jaws; and thou hast brought me into the dust of death." (Psalm 22:14–15).

Of all the things He could have described about His dysfunctional, dying body, it is significant that He said, "All my bones are out of joint." Now, this can certainly be applied to the body of Christ at large and the functionality or lack thereof of the Church; however, it certainly applies to the body of your marriage relationship also! Each spouse *must* function in their particular place and grace!

Just as in Jesus' physical body, when the joints are out of place in your marriage, you can be sure that the body of your marriage will be sick. It may be in pain or diseased. Your marriage body may even be so disjointed that it is at the point of no longer being able to function. *But...*

> *Each spouse must function in their particular place and grace!*

When each member is in their place "according to the effectual working in the measure of every part, maketh increase of the body unto the edifying of itself in love;" when the diamond in your household of faith knows who and what she is; when she understands her God-ordained and assigned position and abilities; when the husband truly understands her abilities and position and gets out of her way; when he places the highest level of esteem and value possible on his virtuous diamond with which the Lord has blessed him; and when he understands his place and grace....

Then they shall enjoy life as heirs together. For one shall put a thousand to flight but two shall put ten-thousand to flight (Deuteronomy 32:30), because where two or three are gathered together in Jesus' name, then God is in the midst of it (Matthew 18:20). Now you have the wife, the husband, and the "I am" all together. "A person standing alone can be attacked and defeated, but two can stand back-to-back and conquer. Three are even better" (Ecclesiastes 4:12 *TLB*). The *Contemporary English Version* says it this way, "Someone might be able to beat up one of you, but not both of you. As the saying goes, 'A rope made from three strands of cord is hard to break.'" It's Mr. and Mrs. Smith plus the Almighty God! It is time for the diamond to live out Isaiah 54. Build that foundation by consulting with the Lord, putting His declarations in your mouth. Mark your territory and build your home.

Shine, diamond, shine.

ISAIAH 54 WEETER EXPANDED TRANSLATION

In Isaiah 54, the Lord is talking to the woman. Utilizing the definitions of the words and expounding on each meaning, here is what Isaiah 54 means, "I swear a most solemn oath to you that no matter what you have been through or are dealing with now, I will not be angry with you or rebuke or yell at you. I promise you that even if the mountains would disappear, and there would be no more hills, still my kindness toward you would be in full force. Not only that but my blood sworn oath to you for my peace will always be intact and I will never break it for I have great, never-ending mercy toward you my daughter!

"You may have been attacked and treated terribly. You may have been pounded with one wave of life right after another, over and over. Just as you recovered from one thing, another came along and knocked you off your feet, pulling you under until you felt like you were drowning all throughout your life. You may have been told your entire life that you're no good and will never amount to anything, without one comforting word being spoken to you.

"But look here and let me show you what I'm going to do through you going forward!

"I am going to make you a diamond in your very own home! If you will allow Me, I will fashion and form you into a most exquisite, multifaceted diamond of the highest quality, cut, and clarity. You will have such clarity that you will be able to see how to use various other gems and elements that I will show you to build your dream home full of wealth and riches. I am personally going to set you securely and steadfastly in your setting so as to bring out your maximum shine and brilliance!

"You and I are going to sit down together and I am going to personally share My wisdom, insight, and understanding with you. I am going to show you how to build the most beautiful and successful life and home that you can imagine. You will have to do the building, but don't worry, I have the master plans

Isaiah 54 Weeter Expanded Translation

and blueprints showing you exactly what to do every step of the way.

"I will give you the words that you will use to lay the very foundations of your home, raise up the walls, and install the windows! You will use the power and authority in My words by declaring them to build impregnable gates and borders that no enemy can breach. I'll show you how to mark your territory. You will indelibly engrave your borders and gates with My mark with your declarations and then defend our territory with whatever firepower necessary to overcome any foe who would dare attempt to enter without your permission.

"I am going to make you a diamond in your very own home!"

"I have equipped you with everything needed to build your home in such a manner to where it is an impenetrable fortress. Don't misunderstand me, oppression, fear, and terror will still bluster and blow around on the outside. Lions will still roam around trying to find a way in, but if you will listen to me, I will show you how to stand firm and give you the weapons to forcefully keep them out.

"Don't be worried if you forget something I've said or you didn't listen and you get a crack in a gate or border through which an enemy is able to get in to your home. If you just stay with me and keep listening, I can fix any breech and deal with any attack at any time. I am not only your Father, I am Almighty God!

"Not only will I make your home, through you, the ultimate fortress against your enemies but it will be such a safe haven for your family. Once everything is in place, you will teach your children how to do the same thing. You will teach them of Me and how to commune with Me and I will teach them the things of the Kingdom just as I have with you. I will see to it that your children have great peace, great financial abundance, great health, long life, and great success throughout their lives in every area!

"You are My own daughter who has chosen to serve Me and this is your heritage and inheritance!"

CONFESSIONS AND PRAYERS

As we saw throughout this book, it is extremely important to declare and pray over your spouse in faith! This principle is set forth in Mark 11:22–25:

> "And Jesus answering saith unto them, Have faith in God. For verily I say unto you, That whosoever shall say unto this mountain, Be thou removed, and be thou cast into the sea; and shall not doubt in his heart, but shall believe that those things which he saith shall come to pass; he shall have whatsoever he saith. Therefore I say unto you, What things soever ye desire, when ye pray, believe that ye receive them, and ye shall have them. And when ye stand praying, forgive, if ye have ought against any: that your Father also which is in heaven may forgive you your trespasses."

In keeping with this vital principle and tool in your endeavor to improve your marriage relationship or maintain the outstanding one you already have, I have provided you with scriptural confessions and prayers to utilize. The Word of God is, after all, medicine to your flesh—your body—and applied daily for maintenance care and three times a day for a dysfunctional body. If symptoms worsen, double the dosage! I hope you get my point.

💎 Love 💎

This should be confessed in faith twice: First, placing "I" in the blanks, then again with your spouses' name placed there!

_____ endures long and is patient and kind; _____ never is envious nor boils over with jealousy, is not boastful or vainglorious, does not display myself/herself/himself haughtily. _____ is not conceited (arrogant and inflated with pride); _____ is not rude (unmannerly) and does not act unbecomingly. _____ does not insist on my/her/his own rights or my/her/his own way, for I/she/he is not self-seeking; I/she/he is not touchy or fretful or resentful; I/she/he takes no account of the evil done to me/her/him [pays no attention to a suffered wrong]. _____ does not rejoice at injustice and unrighteousness, but rejoices when right and truth prevail. _____ bears up under anything and everything that comes, is ever ready to believe the best of every person, my/her/his hopes are fadeless under all circumstances, and I/she/he endures everything [without weakening]. _____

never fails [never fades out or becomes obsolete or comes to an end]. (1 Corinthians 13:4–8 *AMPC*)

I cease not to give thanks for _____, making mention of her/him in my prayers; that the God of our Lord Jesus Christ, the Father of glory, may give unto them the spirit of wisdom and revelation in the knowledge of him: The eyes of their understanding being enlightened; that they may know what is the hope of his calling, and what the riches of the glory of his inheritance in the saints, and what is the exceeding greatness of his power toward _____, according to the working of his mighty power, which he wrought in Christ, when he raised him from the dead, and set him at his own right hand in the heavenly places and hath raised _____ up together, and made her/him sit together in heavenly places in Christ Jesus: Far above all principality, and power, and might, and dominion, and every name that is named, not only in this world, but also in that which is to come: And hath put all things under _____ feet, and gave Jesus to be the head over all things to _____, which is his body, the fulness of him that filleth all in all. And right now the God of peace, that brought again from the dead our Lord Jesus, that great shepherd of the sheep, through the blood of the everlasting covenant, makes _____ perfect in every good work which God predestined (planned beforehand) for her/him [taking paths which He prepared ahead of time], that they should walk in them [living the good life which He prearranged and made ready for them to live], to do his will, working in them that which is well-pleasing in his sight, through Jesus and through His anointing; to whom be glory for ever and ever. Amen. (Ephesians 1:15–23, Hebrews 13:20–21, Ephesians 2:10 *AMPC)*

I do not cease to pray for _____ and to desire that she/he might be filled with the knowledge of God's will in all wisdom and spiritual understanding; that she/he might walk worthy of the Lord unto all pleasing, being fruitful in every good work, and increasing in the knowledge of God; strengthened with all might, according to his glorious power, unto all patience and longsuffering with joyfulness; giving thanks unto the Father, which hath made her/him able to be partakers of the inheritance of the saints in light:

Who hath delivered her/him from the power of darkness, and has translated her/him into the kingdom of his dear Son: In whom they have redemption through his blood, even the forgiveness of sins. (Colossians 1:9–14)

◈ The Husband's Blessing Declaration ◈

In taking my place and role as the head of my wife, I declare over you, _____, be fruitful and multiply and replenish this household! Subdue it and have dominion over everything in this home! Take your place as the diamond in this household of faith and build this home under the instructions and directions of the Master Builder. In doing so, all of the manifestations of the blessing will come on you and overtake you.

Blessed shall you be in the city and blessed shall you be in the field. Blessed shall be the fruit of your body and the fruit of your ground and the fruit of your beasts, the increase of your cattle and the young of your flock. Blessed shall be your basket and your kneading trough. Blessed shall you be when you come in and blessed shall you be when you go out. The Lord shall cause your enemies who rise up against you to be defeated before your face; they shall come out against you one way and flee before you seven ways.

The Lord shall command the blessing upon you in your storehouse and in all that you undertake. And He will bless you in the land which the Lord your

God gives you. The Lord will establish you as a people holy to Himself. And all people of the earth shall see that you are called by the name [and in the presence of] the Lord, and they shall be in awe of you and afraid of you. And the Lord shall make you have a surplus of prosperity, through the fruit of your body, of your livestock, and of your ground, in the land which the Lord swore to your fathers to give you. The Lord shall open to you His good treasury, the heavens, to give the rain of your land in its season and to bless all the work of your hands; and you shall lend to many nations, but you shall not borrow. And the Lord shall make you the head, and not the tail; and you shall be above only, and you shall not be beneath. (Deuteronomy 28:3–13 *AMPC)*